PROM
The Big Night Out

Jill S. Zimmerman Rutledge

TWENTY-FIRST CENTURY BOOKS / MINNEAPOLIS

IN LOVING MEMORY OF HAROLD ETTINGER AND SHELLEY RODIN
BUNTMAN, DEAR HIGH SCHOOL FRIENDS—J.Z.R.

Acknowledgments: Thank you to Susan Cohen; Domenica Di Piazza; Sandy Shanken Woycke; Betty and Garfield Rawitsch; The 10 Twenty-somethings; and as always and forever, to Bob

Twenty-First Century Books
A division of Lerner Publishing Group, Inc.
241 First Avenue North
Minneapolis, MN 55401 USA

Main body text set in Adrianna 11/15.
Typeface provided by Chank.

For reading levels and more information, look up this title at www.lernerbooks.com.

Library of Congress Cataloging-in-Publication Data

Names: Zimmerman Rutledge, Jill S., author.
Title: Prom / by Jill S. Zimmerman Rutledge, LCSW.
Description: Minneapolis, MN : Twenty-First Century Books, 2017. | Audience: Grade 9 to 12. | Audience: Age 13 to 18. | Includes bibliographical references and index.
Identifiers: LCCN 2016009114 (print) | LCCN 2016020367 (ebook) | ISBN 9781512402674 (lb : alk. paper) | ISBN 9781512428506 (eb pdf)
Subjects: LCSH: Proms--Juvenile literature.
Classification: LCC GV1746 .Z55 2017 (print) | LCC GV1746 (ebook) | DDC 793.3/808837318--dc23

LC record available at https://lccn.loc.gov/2016009114

Manufactured in the United States of America
1-39045-21037-5/3/2016

CONTENTS

A PROM STORY

Before cell phones had cameras and before Instagram, communication between girls regarding their "prom looks" had much room for confusion, misunderstandings, and forgetfulness. So once upon a time, a few weeks before her prom, a lovely teen girl found a dress that she absolutely loved. She was extremely happy and told her BFF about the dress. She described her dress in much detail and told her friend that she had bought it at Saks Fifth Avenue. From that exciting conversation, her friend remembered that the dress was green.

A few days later, the friend went shopping for her own prom dress at Saks Fifth Avenue with her mom. The friend found a dress that she absolutely loved. The dress had a long white skirt and a green and white bodice. The dress looked very nice on her, and her mom liked it too. Even though the dress had some green in it, she did not think that it was the same dress as her BFF's. So she didn't think twice about buying it.

You can probably guess what happened. The two friends showed up at prom in the same dress. And the embarrassed friend, who felt guilty about her mistake for years, was me.

Decades later, my BFF Sandy and I laugh about this. Sometimes we even buy the same clothes intentionally—a long, lavender linen skirt; a navy top; and numerous pieces from a favorite designer. We've transformed our prom drama into a life-long bond. Somehow the whole experience has become hilarious and will forever be a thread in the tapestry of our friendship. We have many of "our" clothes hanging in our respective closets. Now, it's fun to buy the same dress.

•••

As I start to write this book, it is prom season. Social media and cell phones are alive with images of fancy dresses, tuxedos, shoes, and bags. The mistake I made would be unlikely—and probably unforgivable—today, as teens have myriad ways to share their prom looks to ensure that not one of their friends will look like them on their big night out. A girl's choice of clothing, shoes, hair, and makeup—and her date's often complementary choice of clothing, hair, and accessories—is a special statement: "This is me, and this is what I am wearing to express myself at my prom."

Twenty-first-century proms have a uniqueness that sets them apart from proms of past generations, where teens worked hard to fit in. So whether you are looking forward or backward to your first high school prom, I hope this book gives you a fun glimpse into the history of proms, from the first proms of the late nineteenth century to the proms of the new millennium.

CHAPTER ONE

AS TIMES GO BY:
PROMS OF THE PAST

People married young in the nineteenth century. Marriages of couples who were in their twenties were the norm. But young men and women from the American upper class couldn't marry just anyone. Rigid social rules of the time dictated that they must marry within their social class. To make sure their children were suitably matched in matrimony, upper-class American parents presented their daughters of marriageable age to society through the rite of a grand ball. Usually in their mid to late teens, girls "made their debut," or their launch into society, at these formal parties, where they could meet male suitors appropriate to their social class. The balls were called debutante or cotillion balls, and one of the first was held in Savannah, Georgia, in 1817.

By the early twentieth century, debutante balls were common in American upper-class society. Newspapers and magazines, such as *Ladies' Home Journal* and *Harper's Bazaar*, covered the events. These media piqued the curiosity of middle-class girls and their mothers who were interested in—and even sometimes obsessed with—pictures of the gorgeous gowns and hairstyles of the debutantes. The media also exposed the American female middle class to the debutantes' poise and to proper social manners, which were considered chic and glamorous at the

Debutante balls were common in nineteenth-century America as a way for upper class families to introduce their daughters to potential marriage partners. The balls, also known as cotillion balls or coming-out parties, are still held in some parts of the United States.

time. In fact, the era's etiquette expert, Emily Post, wrote a book, *Etiquette in Society, in Business, in Politics and at Home*, that included a long chapter about proper social manners at debutante balls. For example, Post advised girls on how to politely let a boy know that they did not want to dance with him.

Like upper-class parents in the early twentieth century, middle-class American parents wanted their children to be well mannered, poised, and beautiful. Proms were invented as a less expensive alternative to debutante balls so that middle-class young people of marriageable age could dress in their finest clothes, have dinner, dance, and practice social etiquette. So the first proms were debutante balls for the masses, a democratization of a high-society rite for young people, both boys and girls. Social etiquette and cultural customs were passed on from the upper class to the middle class in different ways during the early twentieth century, and attending the gala event of prom was one of those.

According to historians, the word *prom* comes from the French word *promenade*, or "a slow walk," in which guests present themselves, often in pairs, at the beginning of a formal event such as a high-society ball. Even in the twenty-first century, some high school proms begin with a grand march, a modern version of the promenade.

THE ROARING TWENTIES

The very first known reference to prom can be found in the biography of Massachusetts resident and Amherst College student Dwight Morrow, who wrote in June 1884, "I have been invited over to the Smith [College] Junior Prom." Proms were first documented as college social events in the late nineteenth century, and they eventually filtered down to high school dances in the 1920s. This era of prosperity, in which many Americans embraced jazz and other daring, new popular trends, was known as the Jazz Age of the Roaring Twenties. By the late 1920s, many proms had become extravagant, annual high school banquets, where students dined and danced the Charleston as big bands played the popular songs of the time. For example, in 1929, just before the stock market crash that brought on the Great Depression (1929–1942), a high school in Massachusetts had a

In the 1920s, teen and adult Americans alike went wild for the Charleston. Women who did the dance were known as flappers, in part because of the way they flapped their arms as they danced. Here, Charles Hoff, a pole vault champion, dances with Tempest Stevens in a 1926 Charleston contest.

prom "with decorations rumored to be the most beautiful ever seen for any social function in town . . . the students danced to such tunes as 'Tiger Rag' and 'Mean To Me' . . . Miss Loretta Giblin of Worcester performed a specialty number . . . a fan dance and a snappy tap dance. Ice cream was served at intermission. The evening was a big success."

THE DEPRESSION AND THE WAR YEARS

The economic crisis of the Great Depression put millions of Americans out of work. Banks closed, businesses failed, and many jobless Americans could not afford to feed their families or pay the rent. So, many young Americans had to take odd jobs, such as delivering newspapers or selling homemade crafts, to help support their families. Others left home to find work in other cities or in other states to support themselves. Thousands of young vagabonds traveled the country by hitching rides on trains and using their street smarts and ingenuity to keep themselves alive.

Vagabond youth did not attend school. Yet high school enrollment and graduation rates actually increased during the 1930s. Since jobs were scarce, the teens who lived at home with their families had little choice but to go to school. According to Howard P. Chudacoff, professor of American social history, by 1940, 49 percent of American teens

In the 1930s, "we were thinking about food on the table. There was no money to spend on a fancy prom. No one had any money. There were proms, but it was all simple and proper, nothing more. Our parents drove us. Our dresses were nothing special."

—Anonymous woman, e-mail to author, June 9, 2015

were graduating from high school, up from 30 percent in 1930. As more American teens went to high school and as public schools sprouted in urban and rural areas around the country, a youth culture began to take root. Teens of all classes—upper, middle, and working—began to meet and spend time together, in classrooms and on school grounds. As boys and girls spent more time together in groups and less time with their families, parents and psychologists became concerned about the emotional upheaval and heightened sexuality of adolescents. They worried that teens would have sex and babies outside of marriage, which was considered totally taboo at that time. Professionals began to encourage middle-class parents and schools to provide supervised activities such as school dances to aid in the "moral development" of teens. Many families, even those who could not pay for fancy prom attire, supported the idea of prom as a healthy activity for maturing teens. Proms soon became a key experience in high school life.

1940s Prom Dos and Don'ts

Proper prom etiquette and morals have changed a lot over the decades. For example, in the wartime years of the 1940s, guys wore suits and girls wore evening dresses to prom. Guys poured the punch for the girls and were expected to know just how much was the right amount to pour into the cup. Girls were expected to chat—but not too much—with their dates. They also knew to wait for the guys to open and close the passenger-side car door for them, and kissing good night at the end of the evening was a definite no-no—at least on the first date. Shaking hands was the way to go.

Many young people in the 1940s got married right out of high school, so prom was a significant rite of passage into adulthood and marriage. In the twenty-first century, prom can be stressful, but there's no longer pressure to marry your prom date. And no one will scold you for not shaking hands at the end of the evening or for jumping in and out of the car on your own!

World War II (1939–1945) brought an end to the Great Depression. The US military sent millions of soldiers and nurses to the battlefields of Europe and Asia. The American home front buzzed with economic activity. Manufacturers that had once built cars and clothing for everyday life began to turn out tanks and other military equipment, uniforms, and other necessities of war. With so many young men off at war, American women joined the workforce in large numbers. For most adolescents during World War II, the high school prom signified a last breath of freedom. Students knew that after high school graduation, they would be thrust into the adult world. For example, boys joined the armed forces right after they graduated from high school, and most girls immediately went to work to support the war effort.

FITTING IN DURING THE 1950S

The word *teenager* became increasingly common in the United States during and after World War II. The word put the focus on young people as a group that had "their own jargon, music, clothes and recreation." Teenagers were a new consumer category. With newspaper delivery and other part-time jobs that were available during the war, teens had money to spend on vinyl phonograph records, bobby socks, saddle shoes, outlandish zoot suits with long jackets—and of course, proms.

After World War II, the US economy boomed. The 1950s was an era of middle-class economic abundance in the United States. Returning veterans and young women were eager to marry and raise families. The vets used government loans to go to college and to buy houses in new and growing suburbs. Families purchased new appliances, televisions, and cars and shopped for the latest fashions. The birthrate soared, giving rise to the baby boom. Dwight D. Eisenhower, the commanding general of US forces in Europe during World War II, was elected president of the

United States, and hopes for peace and prosperity abounded. The teenagers of the 1950s were flooded with television and print images advertising the new affluence of the "happy" Eisenhower years.

Hollywood movies and teen magazines glamorized stars such as Elizabeth Taylor, Natalie Wood, Rock Hudson, and James Dean. These images, along with the prosperity of the times, encouraged teens to buy the things they needed to emulate their movie star idols. Consequently, prom dresses of the 1950s were not just middle-class replicas of expensive debutante gowns. They were more often copies of the glamorous gowns of Hollywood movie stars. According to Deana Case of the LoveToKnow website, prom dresses "were often adorned with sequins, rhinestones, lace, and embroidered appliqués . . . [and] made from fabrics such as organza, taffeta, tulle, and satin. The colors of the 50s prom dresses [were] also unique. Turquoise and tangerine are not often seen in prom dresses from other eras. The body of the

Life magazine documented the Mariemont High School prom (*right*), which took place in 1958 near Cincinnati, Ohio. The prom lasted more than twenty-four hours and included a progressive dinner followed by a formal dance, a riverboat cruise, and breakfast at the school the next morning. After that, students went to an amusement park, and some chose to continue the dance party that evening.

Prom Dresses

Prom dresses from the 1950s are available for sale online and in vintage stores. One of the most popular designers of the 1950s was Christian Dior, who was famous for his New Look dress. It had a cinched waist and a ballet-length full skirt that reached to the middle of the calf or just above the ankle. Prom dresses of the 1950s copied this look.

Model Suzy Parker wears a gathered chiffon bodice and a tulip-pleat skirt, designed by Christian Dior. The Dior New Look, with the classic cinched waist, was extremely popular in the 1950s, both for everyday wear and for formal events such as prom. Horst P. Horst, a famous German American fashion photographer of the era, took this photo.

dress [was] usually fitted and the skirt [was] usually large and 'poofy'. . . . This . . . look [was] feminine, innocent, and glamorous."

Many women who went to prom in the 1950s still remember their dresses. One woman recalls that her 1958 prom dress was long and strapless and made from white eyelet fabric. It had a wide yellow sash that tied in back. She loved the dress and is convinced that "the Dress" is still the most important thing for girls at prom.

Gender roles in the 1950s were essentially unchanged from past generations. Social customs taught girls to wait for boys to open car doors, and boys were expected to be "manly" and pay for the prom tickets and dinners. "Going steady"—the teen version of a monogamous dating relationship—was popular in the 1950s. In fact, going steady was so important in some high schools that many girls were afraid that if by prom time they hadn't received a boy's class ring or a silver pin from a boy—signs of going steady—they couldn't go to the prom. For some couples, "prom was like a junior wedding"—and prom was reserved for heterosexual couples only. Lesbian, gay, bisexual, transgender, and queer/questioning (LGBTQ) couples were not accepted during this era of social conservatism.

CHANGING TIMES

However, the seeds of youth rebellion began to take root during the 1950s. Rock-and-roll music, an offshoot of rhythm and blues, exploded onto the teenage scene, and boys and girls loved to dance to its strong beat. The term *rock and roll* was first used in the early 1950s by Alan Freed, a radio disc jockey in Cleveland, Ohio. The term was also used on the street as a slang term for dancing or sex or both.

Rock and roll is generally attributed to black musicians, such as Cab Calloway and Big Joe Turner, of the 1930s and 1940s, who were influenced by blues and gospel music. While black musicians wrote and recorded many of the first rock-and-roll songs, white artists such as Elvis Presley and Bill Haley & His Comets covered, or rerecorded, them for a mainstream audience. Radio stations played these covers, which led to huge record sales that were not usually financially beneficial to the original black artists.

Popular television shows such as Dick Clark's *American Bandstand* featured teens doing the latest rock-and-roll dance crazes, including the Stroll, the Chalypso (a combination of the cha-cha and calypso), and a line dance called the Madison. Later in the 1950s, rock-and-roll music entered the prom dance scene. Slow dancing to love ballads remained popular too.

The mid-1960s through the mid-1970s were turbulent times in the United States. The early 1960s were marked by the conservative, complacent Eisenhower era. But controversial issues such as the Vietnam War (1957–1975), antipoverty legislation, civil rights, and women's rights soon dominated American life. Three political assassinations between 1963 and 1968 (President John F. Kennedy, his brother New York senator Robert F. Kennedy, and civil rights leader Dr. Martin Luther King Jr.) shocked and saddened teenagers and adults alike. Almost overnight, traditional American assumptions about society were upset. By the mid-1960s, many teens of the era had become members of the counterculture, a youth movement that was primarily antiwar, pro-self-expression, and pro-sexual freedom. Teens began to rebel against the conservative status quo values and politics of their parents.

Television began to reflect these new values too. For example, *That Girl* (1966–1971) starred Marlo Thomas as aspiring actress Ann Marie in the first American television show about a single woman who was not a maid and who did not live with her parents. The Beatles, the most influential band of the era, were

Prom at Prospect Heights High School in Brooklyn, New York, in 1954 was racially integrated at a time when integration in public places around the country was not the social norm.

wildly popular among US teens. The British group began its career with songs such as the innocent and wildly successful hit "I Wanna Hold Your Hand," released in 1963. By 1968 they had released sophisticated studio albums with music that was influenced by politics, transcendental meditation, and the drug culture.

The media also focused on the youthquake movement of the 1960s. Coined by Diana Vreeland, *Vogue* magazine's editor in chief, the term *youthquake* referred to the teen-dominated fashion and cultural movement coming across the ocean from London, England. Superstar fashion models such as Twiggy sported the miniskirt, invented and designed by Britain's Mary Quant. Along with Betsey Johnson, an influential American fashion designer of the era, Quant and other designers created dresses and other clothing in psychedelic colors and prints that were must-haves for teens of the era.

Like many social institutions, proms began to change during this era. On the one hand, many proms in the late 1960s and early 1970s held onto the traditions of the 1950s. Prom was still the first formal event most teens had ever attended. At traditional proms, girls wore long, modest dresses and boys wore tuxedos. Prom couples—still heterosexual only—gave each other corsages (for the girls) and boutonnieres (for the boys). Students voted for prom queen, prom king, and their prom court.

On the other hand, proms began to reflect social change. Prom bands played the hip, exciting music of groups such as the Beatles, the Rolling Stones, the Beach Boys, and black Motown artists such as Stevie Wonder, the Supremes, and the Temptations. Couples danced the newest crazes such as the Hullabaloo, the Swim, the Frug, and the Loco-motion. "Mod" promgoers bucked the system to express their individuality and the values of youth culture through miniskirts and go-go boots.

Some hippie-chic girls rejected the traditional long, white prom dress made of tulle or chiffon. Instead, they made their own dresses, featuring velvet, beads, and fringe. Some girls wore inexpensive (costing as little as $1.25) paper pop art dresses in geometrical black and white or paisley patterns to their proms. And some girls, reflecting the second wave of women's liberation, assertively asked boys to prom instead of vice versa.

SHADOW BOOMERS AND YUPPIES

The last wave of the baby boomers, known as the shadow boomers, were born between 1958 and 1964. They went to prom when the Vietnam War was finally ending. Young men who had fought in the war came home but did not receive the same warm welcome from which World War II vets had benefited. Many teens and college students felt the Vietnam soldiers had fought a morally corrupt war, so these students rejected them and their brave service.

The 1970s was also a decade marked by a sluggish economy and oil shortages, which led to a nationwide energy crisis. President Richard Nixon resigned from office in 1974 at the height of the Watergate crisis, in which he was proven to be the brains behind a major scandal involving spying on his political "enemies."

Segregated Proms

Court rulings outlawed racial segregation in US public schools in the 1960s. Yet in the 1970s, even though high schools were integrated, proms were often racially segregated. This was especially true in the South, where white students attended private white-only proms, and black students attended private black-only proms. In fact, in the 1970s, some schools canceled their proms to prevent white and black students from socializing together. Some schools did not integrate their proms until the twenty-first century.

The idealism and hope of the 1960s began to fade. Instead of championing the utopian, antiestablishment ideals of their older brothers and sisters, shadow boomers focused on themselves and enjoying life. Proms of this era featured a wide variety of pop music, including Joni Mitchell, the Eagles, Jackson Browne, and the Jackson 5. Many proms of the late 1970s and early 1980s were disco-themed, reflecting the wildly popular dance music of the era's club scene. Some boys came to disco proms wearing three-piece leisure suits instead of tuxedos. Many girls donned brightly colored short halter dresses, strapless satin dresses, or chiffon tops teamed with high-slit skirts that whirled on the dance floor.

The 1980s was the decade of young upwardly mobile professionals (yuppies). Yuppie Americans had college educations and high-paying jobs. Surveys showed that yuppies were more focused on money than their parents and grandparents had been. With their new wealth, yuppies tended to live in large houses, drive expensive cars, and wear expensive designer clothing. The yuppie consumer culture of the decade was a time of outrageous ostentation for adults and teens who could afford to flaunt their riches.

Teen pop culture of the 1980s was influenced by family-based TV shows such as *Family Ties* and *The Cosby Show*. *Pretty in Pink* was a popular film that took high school life—and prom—as its theme. Cable television service also became more widespread in the 1980s. By far the most popular cable television channel for teens was the music video network, MTV. By the end of the decade, more than half of American households had cable television, which meant that many American teens watched MTV. MTV made megastars out of artists such as Michael Jackson and Madonna, and teens mimicked their dance moves and fashion styles. For example, teen girls experimented with wearing ripped fishnet stockings, lace gloves, and bustiers as tops rather than as an undergarment, just like Madonna. Gen X girls, born between the late 1960s and the early 1980s, cherished the idea of dressing ironically and for their own pleasure instead of following their parents' expectations.

Boys were also influenced by MTV. They emulated the androgynous (gender neutral) styles of pop stars such as Michael Jackson and Prince. Suddenly it was OK for boys to wear sparkly, ornamented jackets and ruffled shirts; big hair; and sexy, tight pants.

Proms were as abundant and extravagant as the yuppie lifestyle. They offered "the opportunity for conspicuous consumption," and couples went wild with their fashion statements. Girls wore their hair big, teased, and full of hair gel and mousse. Prom dresses were poofy and covered with sparkly sequins, feathers, flounces, and bows. Girls didn't need to spend thousands of dollars on a designer dress. They could find an acceptable knockoff at a local department store. Boys' prom looks in the 1980s included dove gray tuxedo suits with pink shirts and multicolored cummerbunds (waist sashes) with matching bow ties and pocket squares.

Prince performs in California in February 1985. He expanded the boundaries of what men could wear, incorporating a wide range of feminized elements—such as ruffles, sparkling fabrics, boas, and the color pink—into his wardrobe, both onstage and off. Some of this freedom began to make its way into the choices young men made for their prom attire.

Building the Case for Same-Sex Couples at Prom

In 1980 Rhode Island teen Aaron Fricke wanted to take his boyfriend Paul Guilbert to the Cumberland High School senior prom at a country club in nearby Massachusetts. The high school principal, Richard Lynch, rejected the request, on the grounds that it would upset other students, parents, and community members and lead to potential violence against Fricke. But Fricke didn't give up.

The year before, Paul Guilbert had also been denied the right to take a male date to the high school's prom. Other students had taunted and harassed Guilbert for seeking permission to do so. Fricke knew of this and had supported his friend's wishes. After Lynch also denied Fricke's request, Fricke took his case to court. His legal team argued that Lynch's decision restricted Fricke's First Amendment right of association, his First Amendment right to free speech, and his Fourteenth Amendment right to equal protection under the law.

Aaron Fricke (*left*) sued for the right to bring his boyfriend Paul Guilbert (*right*) to their 1980 high school prom at the Pleasant Valley Country Club in Sutton, Massachusetts. He won his case in the lawsuit known as *Fricke v. Lynch*. Richard Lynch was the high school principal at the Rhode Island school that Fricke and Guilbert attended. The pair was among the first in the nation to attend prom as an openly gay couple, and they were featured on the cover of *Christopher Street* magazine in 1981.

Fricke won the case, *Fricke v. Lynch*. The court ruled that the school not only had to allow the couple to attend their prom but it had to also provide police protection to ensure their safety. The event was widely publicized, and in 1981, Alyson Publications—which specializes in GLBT fiction and nonfiction—published *Reflections of a Rock Lobster: A Story about Growing Up Gay*, Fricke's book about growing up gay in America and his fight to go to prom as an out gay man.

Even with the *Fricke v. Lynch* victory, the right to attend prom with a same-sex date was decades from full acceptance in American high schools. Students continue to push, and more victories happen every year. However, LGBTQ students still face discrimination about whom they bring to prom and how they want to dress for the big night. The American Civil Liberties Union (ACLU) and GLAAD (Gay and Lesbian Alliance Against Defamation) are among the many organizations that help protect the rights of LGBTQ teens and adults alike—even at prom.

TiGHTENiNG THE BELT

In the early 1990s, a recession hit the United States and the economy slowed down dramatically. Many families had to tighten their belts and rein in the spending to which they had become accustomed. Families shopped at discount chains to save money, and teens and young adults found it more difficult to get jobs. Grunge bands, such as Nirvana, joined Metallica and Guns N' Roses as rock bands that reflected the restless, unsettled feelings of teens who felt they had no future due to the poor economic climate. So did Public Enemy, Notorious B.I.G., and other hip-hop and rap groups. Influenced by African oral tradition, hip-hop and rap became popular with middle-class teen audiences as expressions of disillusionment and discontent. Ironically, prom movies such as *She's All That* (1999), *10 Things I Hate about You* (1999), and *Never Been Kissed* (1999) romanticized prom as a time to be young, beautiful, and carefree.

The 1990s was a frugal era—and prom looks changed accordingly. Out were the excessively frilly, poofy, colorful dresses of the 1980s. In were more streamlined, simpler, and often black dresses. Teen boys copied a more minimalistic look popularized by male movie stars: a plain-neck shirt with a small stand-up collar. Hairstyles also became less gaudy and flashy. Big hair was replaced by tamer styles, and many girls went to prom wearing a simple, sleek, long ponytail or a neat chignon (bun). Boys could choose among floppy haircuts, short cap-style cuts, or shaved styles influenced by hip-hop musicians. Prom was still an important high school experience in the 1990s, but expectations were toned down—only to be reconfigured again in the new millennium.

CHAPTER TWO
MODERN TIMES:
PROMS FROM THE MILLENNIUM TO THE PRESENT

In 2015 openly lesbian high school honor student Claudetteia Love was barred from wearing a tuxedo to her Carroll High School prom in Monroe, Louisiana. Her principal said the school's dress code did not allow girls in tuxes and that the decision was not personal. When the city's school board president learned about Claudetteia's situation, he supported a change in the dress code to allow Claudetteia to wear whatever she wanted to her prom. Claudetteia said, "I am thankful that my school is allowing me to be who I am." Asaf Orr, a staff attorney at the National Center for Lesbian Rights, which had offered to represent Love at no charge in the event of a lawsuit, supported her position. Orr said, "Participating in [prom] as your whole self, that's really what it's about. These kids are saying 'I want to go to [prom and] I'm not going to hide part of who I am.'"

> "Participating in [prom] as your whole self, that's really what it's about. These kids are saying 'I want to go to [prom and] I'm not going to hide part of who I am.'"
>
> —Asaf Orr, National Center for Lesbian Rights

Aniya Wolf (*left*) and her date (*right*) arrive at William Penn Senior High School's prom in May 2016. The principal of Wolf's Catholic high school had threatened to call the police when Aniya arrived at her school's prom wearing a tux. She accepted an invitation from Brandon Carter, the principal of William Penn Senior High School in York, Pennsylvania, to attend that school's prom instead. Carter said, "We do embrace all."

Like Claudetteia, millennials (people born between 1981 and the late 1990s) and the Generation Zs (born in the years between the mid-1990s and the 2010s) have created their own brand of proms. Their twenty-first-century proms reflect confidence, open-mindedness, self-expression, and sometimes outrageous and over-the-top creative extravagance. These proms are influenced by Internet-infused pop culture, movies, and social media.

For example, blogs, websites, and other social media offer tips about everything from how much in advance a boy should ask a girl to prom ("As soon as possible. . . . Mid-December is not too early," according to the Proms Plus! website) to whether you should get your makeup done for prom (no, if you want to look like yourself; yes, if you want to wow everyone, also according to Proms Plus!). The *Teen Vogue* website offers a wide range of information, including prom personality quizzes, tips on what type of fragrance to wear to prom, and how to dress daringly (tuxedos or short dresses for girls) or like a hopeless romantic (in a long, flowing gown to flatter a girl's complexion).

Prom Movies

Popular prom-themed movies released between 1999 and 2013 include these:

- *Never Been Kissed* (1999). To research an article, a journalist enrolls in her former high school, where she may have a chance to redo everything, even prom.

- *Ten Things I Hate about You* (1999). Leading up to prom, a new boy at school must find someone willing to date the meanest girl in school—the older sister of the girl he has a crush on.

- *She's All That* (1999). A high school jock makes a bet that he can turn an unattractive girl into the school's prom queen.

- *Drive Me Crazy* (1999). A high school girl must find a substitute date to escort her to prom.

- *Bart Got a Room* (2008). Danny desperately searches for a prom date, while the school's biggest loser easily finds a date and a hotel room too.

- *Prom* (2011). A group of teenagers prepare for their high school prom with plenty of drama and high emotions.

- *Teen Spirit* (TV movie, 2011). Amber, a mean yet popular girl, dies after being electrocuted. She is not allowed to enter heaven unless she helps the least popular girl in school become prom queen.

- *Footloose* (2011). A teen boy moves from the city to a small town where rock music and dancing have been banned. His rebellious personality leads to a very interesting prom.

- *Carrie* (2013). This reimagining of the classic 1976 horror film of the same name is based on a 1974 novel by Stephen King. The films and the novel tell the story of Carrie White, a shy girl who is shunned by her peers and overly protected by her religious mother. At prom Carrie uses her mental powers to terrify the party.

Tumblr has a huge choice of prom pictures to scrutinize and emulate. The Golden Asp Prom website has a pull-down tab where you can view customers in their prom dresses. YouTube has video tutorials on prom hairstyles and makeup application, and Pinterest has posts to help with decisions about eye makeup.

Not to worry, guys—there's advice out there for you too! Find tips online about looking your best, acting like a gentleman, and generally having a fun time on your big night. But while the experts have some great tips, remember that your peers around the world are always generating content online. Be sure to utilize resources such as Instagram, YouTube, Vine, and other sites bustling with pre-prom and prom activity, at least some of which will be focused on tips and ideas for the fellows.

For some prom advice specifically aimed at guys, check out "A Young Man's Guide to Prom" at the Art of Manliness website. The guide focuses on what to do and not do at prom. For example, *do* make dinner reservations beforehand; *don't* worry about renting a limo. This page also includes a video on how to dress for prom from the Real Men Real Style website. All your prom questions are answered.

PROMPθSALS

Proms can be very expensive—sometimes prohibitively so. Teens and their families spend hundreds of dollars on clothing, food, flowers, transportation, and after-parties. Yet according to a 2015 survey by Visa, total average prom expenses have actually decreased in the past few years, from an average of $1,139 in 2013 to an average of $919 in 2015.

Prom costs are dependent on where you live. If you live in the northeastern United States, the average prom night expense is $1,169. If you live in the West, the expense is $937. In the South, the expense is $849, and if you live in the Midwest, the cost is closer to $733.

Studies show that as much as one-third of the total cost of prom goes for the promposal. The best insurance for a successful promposal is when the inviter is sure the invitee will say yes.

Sometimes people in relationships stage promposals for the fun of it. For example, a girl may know that the person she is dating will ask her to prom, but she doesn't know when and how. Other times the inviter will check with friends of the invitee to see if that person would want to be the inviter's prom date before orchestrating a promposal. Teens often post videos of their promposals on social media. It's a way to be seen and admired, a way to garner as many Likes as possible, and a way to improve social standing and to temporarily bolster self-esteem.

Journalist Miriam Jordan of the *Wall Street Journal* describes a particularly fantastic promposal: Uma, a sixteen-year-old girl, was visiting a college thousands of miles from home. "Suddenly, a horn blast pierced the air and six young men emerged from behind [a] church's pillars. Four of them unfurled a huge banner that popped 'the question.' Another raised a giant photo of Kell . . . the guy who had enlisted their help from 2,500 miles [4,023 kilometers] away. Still another accomplice captured the proceedings on video . . . 'Uma, prom with Kell?' the banner read."

THE DOWNSIDE

But promposals can have a downside. Some teens expect an elaborate promposal and may not say yes if they are asked to prom without one. As reporter Emanuella Grinberg of CNN says, "For some girls (and some boys), not getting a promposal is their worst nightmare. And yet being approached with flowers in the hallway can be a letdown, especially if a friend was serenaded in a flash mob."

If the answer is no, the inviter can experience public embarrassment, which can lead to low self-esteem and depression. It is one thing to be disappointed when a girl or boy says no on the phone. It is a whole different level of stress, anxiety, and humiliation for a person to say no in a public venue— and to have the no immediately broadcasted to the entire school via social media. The flip side is that girls and boys may feel pressure to say yes to a promposal for fear of being labeled mean or "a bitch," even if they do not want to be the promposer's date.

Some teens are not enamored of the promposal. In fact, some think that the whole idea is excessive and may not always be done with authenticity. Isidro sums up his feelings this way: "I can see how [promposals] are becoming more popular in this viral age, but making a whole production out of it doesn't necessarily make them genuine. Sincerity trumps showmanship."

THE PROM DRAFT

One controversial prom practice is the prom draft, in which a group of boys privately create a draft pool of girls to ask to prom and rank their desirability. The group posts its rankings online so that the entire school can see the results. The boys then pay for and pick numbers through a lottery, pro football style, choosing their prom dates from the draft pool. Some people, including girls, see this as a fun way to organize prom dates. Yet most students, teachers, and mental health professionals think that it is a form of female objectification and sexual harassment, which can lead to and encourage low self-esteem, poor body image, and social anxiety in girls.

Parry Aftab, a cyberbullying expert, lawyer, and director of WiredSafety, an organization that helps teens stay safe online, says, "The thing that's most surprising to me is that girls are going along with this [prom draft]. The fastest way to shut it down [prom drafts] is for the girls to turn around and say, 'I won't be sold. . . . I'm worth more than that."

INTEGRATED PROMS

Millennials and Gen Zers generally believe in the positive power of diversity, and they put their beliefs into practice at prom. For example, many American high schools have held their first racially integrated proms in the twenty-first century. Actor Morgan Freeman, the most famous graduate of Charleston High School in Charleston, Mississippi, sponsored the first integrated prom at his alma mater in 2008. The school had been integrated in 1970, but proms there remained racially segregated. Freeman offered to pay for an integrated prom in the 1990s, but the school did not accept the offer until many years later. The first integrated prom at Charleston was the subject of the documentary *Prom Night in Mississippi,* which debuted at the Sundance Film Festival in 2009. At Vidalia High School in Georgia, seniors took a stand against segregated proms that same year. *Seventeen* magazine published an article on the prom, telling readers that "seniors like Melissa, 18 . . . and her friends and fellow student government members stepped in: 'Our senior class is so tight-knit, and [we] felt it would be so much more memorable to finally have just one prom for everyone. . . . For a big change to happen, you need to involve lots of people. It wasn't just one person who made this happen; we

For decades, prom at Wilcox County High School in Rochelle, Georgia, was segrated: one dance for white students and one for black students. In 2013 four senior girls, two black and two white, at the school created a Facebook page to ask for support and donations to pay for a prom party that would be open to everyone. Nearly half of the school's students came to prom that year.

got everyone involved, by asking for opinions and getting people to vote on decisions.'"

Also in 2009, photographer Gillian Laub published pictures in the *New York Times Magazine* of segregated proms at Montgomery High School in Georgia. The coverage helped inspire that school's first integrated prom in 2011.

A group of teens at Wilcox County High School in rural Rochelle, Georgia, organized their school's first racially integrated prom two years later, in 2013. Previously the school did not sponsor proms at all. The formal event was instead held privately and was segregated into "white proms" and "black proms." A cohesive group of students, black and white, had the resolve to organize a prom hosted at the school—and open to students of all races. Community leaders criticized the students' efforts initially. Yet relentless social media support, along with community donations of cash, dresses, and DJ services, helped convince school leaders to sponsor an integrated prom that the entire class could attend together. Mareshia Rucker wore a red, sparkly dress to the prom. To commemorate the groundbreaking event, she then donated her dress to the Inspiring Change Gallery of the Canadian Museum for Human Rights in Winnipeg, Manitoba.

LGBTQ PROM COUPLES

In June 2015, the US Supreme Court ruled that same-sex couples can legally marry in every state in the United States. Teens overwhelmingly support this ruling and believe that LGBTQ couples have the right to attend prom.

Among the first openly lesbian couples in the nation to attend prom together was high school senior Heidi Leiter (seventeen) and her date, college student Missy Peters (twenty). In 1991 the couple went to Heidi's Osbourn High School senior prom in Manassas, Virginia, dressed in high heels and tuxedos with lavender sweetheart rose boutonnieres. The two had been dating for two years and had been star athletes on their high school's basketball team.

Family and friends supported Heidi and Missy's courage and conviction. So did many of the students and teachers at the high school. Many national print media sources, including the *Washington Post* and *Glamour* magazine, reported on their story. The young women also made guest appearances on talk shows, and their story was the subject of the 1994 HBO television special *More Than Friends: The Coming Out of Heidi Leiter*, geared especially for middle and high school students. According to a 1994 article in the *Washington Post*, Heidi said that "we didn't do it for the publicity. . . . We went to prom because I was a senior and I wanted to go to prom."

Many LGBTQ teens have not received the same support as Heidi and Missy. For example, in 2010, Constance McMillen wanted to bring her girlfriend to her Itawamba Agricultural High

Eighteen-year-old Constance McMillen, an out lesbian senior at her high school in Itawamba County, Mississippi, fought back after her school announced it wouldn't hold the senior prom in 2010 because she wanted to bring a girlfriend as her date. She also planned to wear a tuxedo to prom. McMillen won her battle.

School prom in Mississippi but was barred by a school board rule stating that prom dates must be of the opposite gender. Constance contacted the American Civil Liberties Union to discuss suing the school for discrimination. In response, the school board canceled the prom altogether, calling Constance's reaching out to the ACLU "a distraction 'to the educational process.'" But Constance won in the end. With the threat of a lawsuit, the school district eventually agreed to create a policy protecting students from discrimination on the basis of sexual orientation and gender identity and to pay Constance $35,000, plus her attorney's fees, which she put away for college. Constance was also featured in *Glamour* magazine, on television, and at the 2010 GLAAD Media Awards for her brave contribution to the rights of LGBTQ teens.

Similarly, in 2014, Anais Celini and her transgender boyfriend, Nathaniel Baez, were denied the right to attend prom at Martin Luther High School, a private Christian high school in Queens, New York. The school told the couple that they could not go to prom because the school considered them a same-sex couple, even though Nathaniel was transitioning from female to male. (The school has a policy forbidding same-sex couples from

The Constitution Protects Us All, Even at Prom

Each year, the ACLU gets calls from teens whose schools refuse to let them bring a same-sex date to prom. Some schools also forbid teens to attend prom unless they wear gender-conforming clothes (dresses for girls, tuxedos for boys). Some schools tell transgender teens that they cannot go to prom. These policies are illegal because they violate the right to free expression guaranteed by the First Amendment of the US Constitution. Several federal court rulings have supported this right. If a school tries to stop people who express LGBTQ identities from going to prom or if a person wants to talk to someone about these issues, they can call (212) 549-2673 or check out the prom resources page at the ACLU website at https://www.aclu.org/prom-resources -lgbt-students.

attending prom.) The couple didn't want to fight the school system, but they also didn't want to let the school's discriminatory decision ruin their special night. So they decided to have their own small prom celebration, and a transitional housing center donated the space for their event. Anais told reporters that "we are no longer a same-sex couple. They need to see [Nathaniel] as male and respect that. We didn't want to sneak ourselves into prom, we wanted to be upfront and respectful about it."

Anais and Nathaniel got secret support from some teachers at Martin Luther High School who were afraid to support them publicly because they feared losing their jobs. The couple received other random acts of kindness from their community. For example, on a trip to the seaside entertainment parks at Coney Island, a vendor who recognized the couple from a report on the local television news treated them to free spray-on tattoos. The Gay, Lesbian & Straight Education Network (GLSEN) also supported them and created an online campaign so that others could send messages of support.

"Prom is a highlight of the school year for many students, and no one should have that opportunity taken away," said Daryl Presgraves, the GLSEN director of communications. "Excluding a student from such a memorable part of the school experience simply for being who they are is not only wrong—it's humiliating. We wish Anais and Nathaniel the best and want them to know they have our full support."

Another prom couple to benefit from the widespread conviction among teens and adults alike that *all* couples should be able to attend their high school proms was Michael Martin and his boyfriend, Logan Westrope. In 2015 the couple went to prom at their West Virginia high school and "'danced together the whole night' . . . [receiving] compliments as they grooved to tunes by Sam Smith, Wiz Khalifa and John Legend." The experience created a great memory. On the way home in the car, Michael told Logan, "This is our last prom and I'm

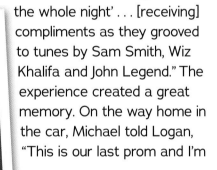

Senior Michael Martin *(left)* and his boyfriend, Logan Westrope *(right)*, went to their high school prom in a small town in eastern West Virginia as an out gay couple in 2015. Michael is a soccer player, and Logan is a tennis player. That same year, the couple told their coming-out and prom story as part of the It Gets Better Project, a series of video interviews from a wide range of individuals to inspire hope among LGBTQ youth around the world who face bullying and other forms of harassment.

so glad I got to spend it with you. . . . I couldn't have asked for a more perfect night."

TRANSGENDER GiRL VOTED PROM QUEEN

Brooklynn Buenaventura was born in a male body, but she always felt that her true self is a girl. She has started the process of transitioning, and even though she says it is scary, she feels brave and wants to let other transgender teens know that it is OK to come out. "I'm not hiding anything, anymore. . . . We're not different," she told a news reporter.

Brooklynn's family has been super supportive, and her friends are proud of her. In fact, they voted her prom queen at the 2015 Renton High School prom in Washington State, where she lives. But Brooklynn said that the best prize of all is that she feels accepted on the outside for what she feels on the inside. She said, "You just have to be who you are, don't be scared to open up."

"You just have to be who you are, don't be scared to open up."

—Brooklynn Buenaventura

CHAPTER THREE

THE DRESS, THE TUX:
CLOTHES TELL A STORY

S tyles come and go, but a girl's dress continues to be one of the most important—and expensive—highlights of prom. In earlier decades, prom dresses emulated the gowns of debutantes. In the twenty-first century, many are inspired by red-carpet celebrity dresses. Some girls even buy dresses that actually could be worn on the red carpet. For example, a girl in Clovis, California, wore a Versace designer dress that cost more than $8,000 to her prom. Of course, most girls and their families are much less extravagant when they purchase their prom dresses. Still, it is not unusual for a girl to spend $1,000 on her dress, shoes, and jewelry.

Prom dresses are often the centerpiece of the evening. Some girls pay thousands of dollars for their dress, while others look gorgeous on a budget. Some even make their own, while others choose to wear a stylish pantsuit instead. This teen chose an evening dress to flatter her shoulders.

For the Girls with Curves

Some smart retailers are catering to girls who have curves. For example, many department stores have cute, reasonably priced prom dresses in sizes 14 to 24. A wide variety of websites also have great ideas for flattering prom dresses of all sizes.

Many girls like to wear one-of-a-kind dresses to prom. Prom dress registries are one way to ensure that no two girls will show up to prom in the same dress. Department stores and boutiques that have prom dress registries will not sell the same dress to more than one girl who is attending a specific prom. "Nobody wants to go to prom and play 'Who wore it better?' with their friends," said a seventeen-year-old girl from New York, who bought her dress at a boutique that features a prom dress registry. "To have someone wear the same dress, it would be embarrassing for both of you," said another girl who bought her prom dress at the same boutique.

Prom dress registries do have a downside. When a girl is told that she cannot buy a dress she loves because someone else has already bought it, she may feel hugely disappointed—and many girls may leave the store in tears. The fear of this type of scenario can set up a competition about prom dresses that exacerbates prom stress for girls. Many girls shop for dresses several months before prom, even before they have a date. Julie Paget, co-owner of a New York boutique, comments that girls "want to lock up their dress before everybody else. . . . The whole thing is done earlier and it's hyped up."

DIY DRESSES!

Do-it-yourself (DIY) dresses are a great creative alternative to the prom dress registry to ensure that your prom look is yours and yours alone. Eighteen-year-old Kyemah McEntyre, from East Orange, New Jersey, was a victim of bullying by some of her high school classmates. But she didn't let the taunting and name-calling define her—she defined herself! With her unbridled energy and artistic talent, she created a gorgeous one-of-a-kind prom dress inspired by her African American identity. On the big night, her classmates were in awe of her beauty and voted her prom queen!

Kyemah posted pictures of herself in her prom dress on Instagram and received ten thousand Likes. She became an overnight Internet sensation and used this platform to speak out against bullying and negativity. She posted this quote with her Instagram pictures: "This is for always being labeled as 'ugly' or 'angry.' Thank God stereotypes are just opinions."

Kyemah says, "As an artist, I have a completely different point of view compared to most individuals. I am extremely analytical and observant. . . ." She added, "Being exposed to all kinds of people and cultures is the muse for my artwork."

Singer-songwriter Naturi Naughton (*right*) attended the 2015 Black Entertainment Television (BET) awards in Los Angeles, wearing a dress designed by eighteen-year-old Kyemah McEntyre. The two women are from East Orange, New Jersey. When Naughton saw the prom dress McEntyre had designed for herself, she invited the teen to create an African-inspired dress for her appearance at the BET awards.

Kyemah's story touched another person from East Orange, actress Naturi Naughton. Naturi was so impressed with Kyemah's work that she commissioned the aspiring artist to design a red-carpet gown for her. Naturi wore her Kyemah McEntyre designer dress to the 2015 Black Entertainment Television (BET) awards. Kyemah will continue her studies at the Parsons School of Design in New York. Her richly colorful, original designs reflect her African heritage—as well as her bright future.

> *"Being exposed to all kinds of people and cultures is the muse for my artwork."*
>
> —Kyemah McEntyre

A STARRY NIGHT DRESS

Julia Reidhead, a high school senior in Mesa, Arizona, loves art and loves to be creative. So in 2014, she designed and sewed her own unique, one-of-a kind prom dress with a famous painting as her inspiration. Julia bought a gently used wedding dress that fit her perfectly and used it as a canvas to hand paint her favorite painting, Vincent van Gogh's *The Starry Night*. With her mom's help, she first

Julia Reidhead designed her own prom dress, using acrylic paints to hand paint a forty-dollar, thrifted wedding dress from which she had removed the train. She first sketched the design, based on Van Gogh's famous *Starry Night* painting (*right*), onto paper before using a pencil to outline the design onto the fabric. Then she began to paint, from the hem up.

removed the train from the dress and practiced on it until she was ready to draw and paint on the dress itself. The dress cost forty dollars and took Julia ten days, or approximately forty-five hours, to paint with acrylic paints. Julia was pleased that the dress already had lace and pearls. She told reporters, "This will make for amazing textures! I'll just paint right over them."

Her date's reaction? "Her dress was beyond amazing!" said Alden Durfee, who took Julia to the prom. He told her, "You will be the talk of the dance!"

A CAMO DRESS

Truck driver David Herron served in the US Air Force—and learned how to sew straight seams there. His seventeen-year-old daughter, Mariah, asked him to make her prom dress. He jokingly agreed. "Next thing I know, I was making her dress," he said.

The Herron family lives in Marshfield, Wisconsin. Herron created the special prom dress out of a camouflage fabric called Snow White Camouflage. White and patterned with black tree limbs and leaves, it perfectly reflected Mariah's love for the outdoors. Herron worked for approximately six weeks to design and sew Mariah's dress. The finished fashion creation was a strapless gown with a thick black tulle ruffle trim on the top and a black satin bow. Mariah was pleased with her dad's creative effort. As Herron told reporters, "She asked me if I'd make her a wedding dress."

AND THE TUX!

Just because a boy wears a tuxedo to prom doesn't mean he has to have a cookie-cutter look. Boys don't have to resemble penguins at prom. Examples of color, creativity, and coolness are practically limitless. Tuxedo jackets and suits may be worn in traditional black, charcoal, or white—or in red, paisley, or animal prints. Bow ties are often worn in a kaleidoscope of colors, but long ties are also in style at twenty-first-century proms. Vests and pocket squares offer a pop of color that may or may not exactly match the color of the tie. Socks are usually black, but shoes range from the traditional black patents to colorful high-tops. Some boys skip ties, vests, and socks altogether. One of the coolest looks on Pinterest in 2016 was a boy in a charcoal tux jacket and vest, light gray tuxedo slacks, a long red tie, a red silk pocket square—and red patent leather shoes! His date had a long, red mermaid dress that complemented his look.

And as everyday and special event outfits become increasingly gender neutral, some teen boys are choosing to blend skirts or dresses into their prom outfits. For example, teen musician Jaden Smith wore a simple white skirt with a loose black top and a black jacket to his 2015 prom. Black leggings and tennis shoes and white fingerless gloves completed the look. His date, actor Amandla Stenberg (of *Hunger Games* fame), wore a sleeveless, floor-length black and gold dress.

Jaden Smith is not the only American male to choose a skirt for a social event. Fashion is becoming more gender neutral, and fashion designers are creating dresses and skirts such as this one worn by a male model *(left)* for men, for social occasions and for everyday wear.

STUCK ON PROM

Since 2001 thousands of high school students have entered a contest for the best prom outfits made of—duct tape. In fact, the Duck Tape brand, based in Avon, Ohio, holds a yearly Stuck at Prom contest with a $10,000 scholarship for the grand prize winners. Six additional category prizes include Best Singles Entry and Best Theme. Contest entrants must make their dresses and tuxes out of the company's brand of duct tape, attend their proms wearing the outfits, and post pictures of themselves in their prom clothes on the Stuck at Prom website for a chance to win.

From 2001 to 2015, teens have used 92,796 rolls of duct tape (equal to 13,919 football fields) for making outfits for girls and boys. They have used eighteen different colors of duct tape, including black, red, pink, turquoise, and neon green. Maroon, electric blue, purple, yellow, and orange are also popular choices. Over the years, the contest has attracted 7,733 entrants, who have spent 386,650 hours (equal to 193,325 two-hour movies) making their outfits. As of 2015, teens have submitted a total of 515,229 votes.

This couple made their prom outfits entirely from duct tape. Thousands of students across the United States and Canada use hundreds of rolls of Duck Tape brand tape every year to compete in the Stuck at Prom competition for best prom outfits. The public votes online, and the winners get a share of $50,000 in college scholarship prizes. This couple was among the top ten finalists in 2014.

RECYCLED PROM WEAR

Not everyone has the desire, talent, time, or creative ideas to make their own prom outfits. And not everyone can afford the hefty price tag for something new. Many community organizations across the United States gather donations of new and gently used prom dresses, tuxedos, and accessories for teens who need help to pay for the high cost of prom.

For a few lucky inner city high school seniors in Los Angeles, California, the *New York Times Magazine* held a prom contest to give eight students "the same treatment given Academy Award nominees: stylist, couture gowns, hair and makeup, stretch limo and heaps of diamonds." Famous fashion designers such as Versace, Valentino, and Armani donated gowns. Hollywood hairstylists, makeup artists, and manicurists helped make the teens feel glamorous and gorgeous for prom. One girl exclaimed, "I wish these eyelashes lived with me!"

Amanda Martinez *(left)* gets help from Anna Plaster *(right)*, the case manager of the Princess Project San Diego, as she searches through donated outfits for a dress to wear to her prom in San Diego, California. The project launched in 2007 and helps thousands of financially challenged teens dress for prom each year.

Prom Goes Green

If you are short on cash and want an amazing dress or tuxedo for prom, check out the following list. Most of these organizations have dresses and tuxes available at the beginning of prom season, so contact them in the early spring for your best choices. If you don't find something close to where you live, do an online search for prom dress donations in your city or town. You'll very likely find something in your area.

- Becca's Closet (Nationwide)
  http://www.beccascloset.org

- Belle of the Ball (New Hampshire, Massachusetts, and Rhode Island)
  http://antons.com/belle/about/

- The Cinderella Affair (Arizona)
  http://www.cinderellaaffair.org/

- Cinderella's Closet (Kentucky, Arkansas, Florida, Georgia, Kansas, North Carolina, Tennessee, Ohio, Pennsylvania, and Wisconsin)
  http://www.cinderellasclosetnky.org

- Operation Glass Slipper (Minnesota and Western Wisconsin)
  http://operationglassslipper.org/

- Operation Pretty and Polished (Washington, DC, Area)
  http://wpgc.cbslocal.com/2015/03/02/operation-pretty-polished-2015/

- Operation Prom (Nationwide)
  http://operationprom.org

- Princess Project (California Based)
  http://princessproject.org/get-a-dress/

- Project G.L.A.M. (New York City, Long Island, New Jersey, Milwaukee, and Los Angeles)
  http://www.wgirls.org/get-involved/project-glam/

- Prom Goes Green (Chicago Area)
  http://promgoesgreen.com

The Cinderella and Prince Charming Project, supported by various corporations and companies, was held in South Los Angeles just before the 2015 prom season. It's a more down-to-earth yet amazing event for teens who might not otherwise be able to afford prom. More than one thousand underprivileged teen boys and girls received free dresses, tuxedos, shoes, and other accessories for prom—and they also got lessons in ballroom dancing from professional dancers. One of the dance instructors, Danielle Jordan, said, "With Cinderella the message is charity, generosity and kindness."

CHAPTER FOUR

MAKING A DIFFERENCE:
PROMS WiTH HEART AND SOUL

Most proms are held at a high school, a hotel, or sometimes a country club or other fancy venue. Groups of friends and their dates may rent buses or limos; plan for after-parties; and spend a lot of money on tickets, dresses, tuxedos, accessories, hair, makeup, corsages, boutonnieres, and manicures and pedicures. The prom is considered the biggest formal occasion of high school, so most promgoers focus on making themselves beautiful and attractive for what they hope will be a fun experience to be remembered always.

But what if the focus of prom was to do something good for others or to support a friend who was paralyzed by a stray bullet or to show the world that even a hurricane as fierce as Katrina can't destroy dreams of a senior prom? This is a side of prom that we don't often hear about, but proms can be creative expressions of unity, courage, and giving to others.

A CELEBRATION OF LIFE

The Memorial Sloan Kettering Cancer Center, a hospital in New York City, has hosted the annual Pediatric Prom since the

Diana Leung, sixteen, partied on the dance floor with her friend Jake Seymer at prom night in 2007. Children's Hospital of Orange County in Orange, California, hosted the event for young patients with cancer. Leung was diagnosed with brain cancer that year. She died in 2011 when she was nineteen.

early 1990s. In the beginning, the dance was a modest party to boost the spirits of the children, teens, and young adults who were hospitalized for cancer treatments. In the twenty-first century, the prom has evolved into an all-out gala, featuring a DJ, balloons, streamers, thrones for the prom queen and prom king, and banquet tables filled with favorite treats such as cupcakes and an all-you-can-eat sundae bar. Wealthy Manhattan socialites and specialty shops such as Promingdales and the Men's Shop donate dresses and tuxedos for the event. Girls and boys get pre-prom pampering with mani-pedis, makeup artists, and face painters. Personal shoppers also help everyone feel special. Even though some promgoers have to be connected to their IVs, and others are too sick to dance, they all agree that the Pediatric Prom is a great way to feel uplifted, forget their cancer for a few hours, feel beautiful and handsome—and celebrate life!

EARTHQUAKE PROM

In 2010 a catastrophic earthquake devastated the island nation of Haiti. That spring the juniors and seniors at Hay Springs High School in Hay Springs, Nebraska, voted to use their prom budget to set up a relief fund for the Haitian earthquake victims. The students had raised more than $5,000 for their prom. Instead of using it for a fancy prom dinner, they put the money in the Haiti relief fund. At their Nebraska prom, the Hay Springs students ate lasagna and brownies baked by teachers and parents.

As word spread about the altruism at Hay Springs High, people in the community offered to donate goods and services so that the students could have a more lavish prom. However, the students asked potential donors to contribute cash donations to their Haiti relief fund instead. As the Hay Springs High School principal said, "We are not spending a dime on prom. . . . If anyone donates money to us for the prom, it will go directly to the [Haiti relief] bank fund." Melanie Wieseler, a math teacher at Hay Springs High said, "I'm sure the prom will be a night to remember. Our students have guaranteed that."Trenton Kuhn, a junior at the high school, agreed. He said, "We just wanted to show people we cared."[3]

> The students had raised more than $5,000 for their prom. Instead of using it for a fancy prom dinner, they put the money in the Haiti relief fund.

A BIG PROM SURPRISE

Alyah Mitchell and J. R. Hall, both high school students from Texas, had planned to go to Alyah's prom as friends in March 2015. But a car accident put J. R. in the hospital six weeks before the prom. Even though the two friends hoped that J. R. would heal quickly, he was still in the hospital at prom time.

So Alyah decided to surprise him. She showed up at his hospital room a couple of hours before prom—all dressed up in her prom dress! Alyah said, "I had talked to him about maybe coming up there just to show him what I look like all dolled up. . . . I wanted to put a smile on his face any way possible, so I thought it would be nice to surprise him." About his reaction, Alyah remembers that "he was super-surprised because he had no idea I was [really] coming!"

Alyah posted a picture of herself and J. R. in the hospital on Twitter. To her surprise, the photo has gotten ten thousand Favorites and six thousand retweets. Alyah went to her high school prom without a date and had a good time with her friends. And since J. R. attended a different high school with a different date, for its she planned to go to his prom later in the year. Alyah and J. R. will most likely always remember her pre-prom surprise as an act of true friendship and kindness.

Alyah and J. R. will most likely always remember her pre-prom surprise as an act of true friendship and kindness.

PROM GODPARENTS

In the fall of 2009, a shutdown Austin, Texas, high school was reopened with a new name, East Side Memorial High. But there was no money in the school budget for a senior prom. Many families were struggling financially and could not help out. It looked as if the class of 2010 would not have the experience of a senior prom, and a tough economy was to blame.

However, one senior girl, Yesika Acuña, didn't want to see this happen. A determined, straight A

In May 2010, *People* magazine featured a story about the efforts of senior Yesika Acuña *(in yellow)*, her mentor Janette Miller *(red floral dress)*, and architect Stefan Molina *(purple shirt)* to bring prom to East Side Memorial High.

student, she sought help from Janette Miller, her mentor through the city's Hispanic Chamber of Commerce. Miller, along with an architect friend, Stefan Molina, raised $6,000 for the prom in cash and in-kind donations, including prom dresses from a local boutique. Through the help of Miller and Molina and the community, East Side Memorial High was able to have a Mardi Gras-themed senior prom. Molina said, "I went to prom and it was special for me and . . . I didn't want these kids to miss out." Yesika said, "Janette and Stefan . . . are godparents to our whole class."

PROM FAiRY GODMOTHERS

Several years earlier, at West Philadelphia High School in Philadelphia, Pennsylvania, a pair of "fairy godmothers" were also committed to helping girls go to prom—girls who could not have afforded to attend otherwise. Athletic director and physical education teacher Patricia Cassano and Elaine Flournoy, a special education teacher, started a program to provide gowns and other resources to girls in need, plus money for parking, pictures, and food. They started the program after learning that girls weren't attending their prom because they couldn't afford to go. Cassano said, "There's only one senior prom. . . . A lot of them [girls] will never dress up like this again, except for a formal wedding. No girl should miss her senior prom."

The "fairy godmothers" asked fellow teachers, businesses, and other people in the community to donate money, dresses, shoes, and costume jewelry. If they weren't able to donate money or clothing, the women asked if people could give a girl a manicure or do her hair instead. "We hit everybody up," said Cassano. "Stuff we [couldn't] wrangle, we [asked] if we [could] have it for half-price, at a discount." And even if the gowns were outdated, the teachers found volunteer dressmakers to make updates with "a hem here, a ruffle there" so that they were in "right-off-the rack condition."

The reward? For Cassano, it is to "see someone who thought they wouldn't be [at the prom] . . . to see them walk through the door, that's it, that's the benefit. What more is there?"

SENiOR PROM

Teens have also reached out to senior citizens to enjoy cross-generational proms. For example, in 2015 high school students in Denver, Colorado, attended a senior prom—at a senior center. The leadership club at Grandview High School dressed up and joined more than eighty senior citizens at the InnovAge Johnson Adult Day Program. This "senior prom" is the biggest social event of the year at the center. Students danced with the older seniors and witnessed the crowning of the center's 2015 prom king, Robert Van Natta, aged eighty, and prom queen, Beverly Owens, aged seventy-four.

Another prom for high school seniors and senior citizens inspired Rahul Peravali. When Peravali attended Houston High School in Germantown, Tennessee, his senior class went to a senior center prom near the school, and according to Peravali, "everybody really had fun."When Peravali arrived that fall at Rhodes College, in Memphis, for his first year of college study, he decided to organize a prom with college students and seniors at the city's J. K. Lewis Senior Center. One hundred students and seventy seniors attended the event. The senior citizens—and the students—loved it. "There was one older man who never sat down. He danced with student after student, having the time of his life," remembered Peravali.

DETERMINED TO DANCE

Being in a wheelchair did not stop Missy Jenkins from attending her prom. Seventeen months after being a victim of a school shooting, she was busy getting ready for her big night at the

Heath High School prom in Paducah, Kentucky. With her twin sister, Mandy, by her side, she got a French manicure, had her eyebrows waxed, and got her hair styled. For her big night, Missy wore a purple crepe dress and a corsage from her date, Barrett.

On prom night, Missy and Barrett had dinner at a seafood restaurant. The only glitch was that they had forgotten to tell the reservationist that Missy was in a wheelchair. Instead of reserving a table for the couple on the first floor, staff had chosen a table on the second floor. When the couple arrived at the restaurant, the staff carried Missy up a flight of stairs to their table. After dinner, the couple headed to the prom dance at the local civic center. They even figured out a way to slow dance: Missy told a reporter later that "we just held hands and kind of swayed." Her friends and family were proud of her determination and bravery.

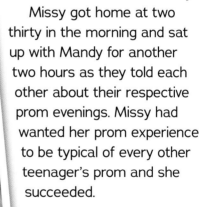

Missy got home at two thirty in the morning and sat up with Mandy for another two hours as they told each other about their respective prom evenings. Missy had wanted her prom experience to be typical of every other teenager's prom and she succeeded.

Missy Jenkins was shot and wounded at Heath High School in Paducah, Kentucky, in 1997 by a fourteen-year-old classmate, who wounded four others and killed three. The next spring, Missy—who is paralyzed and in a wheelchair—went with her date to prom. Several years later, in 2000, Missy was able to walk the final distance of the Los Angeles Marathon wearing her leg brace.

HURRICANE KATRINA

It started with a simple idea that came to her in 2005 during winter finals season as she was looking for a prom dress in the crammed racks at a designer discount store. Hurricane Katrina had recently pounded the Gulf Coast of the southeastern United States, and it dawned on Marisa West, a high school senior at Georgetown Day School in Washington, DC, that many girls would not be able to buy prom dresses because their families had lost everything in the destructive storm. "I was looking through all the sequins and the beads and the glitter and I realized that in New Orleans [Louisiana] so many girls wouldn't feel that joy you feel at prom—all because of the devastation of Katrina. I thought I could help restore at least one of their high school traditions that they wouldn't have otherwise."

So Marisa started a prom dress drive that drew twenty-eight hundred donations from across the country. One man was so touched by the sentiment of the drive that he sent his late wife's formal gowns, as a tribute to her. Girls from a total of ten high schools—nine in New Orleans and one in Bay Saint Louis, Mississippi, were able to choose dresses for their prom in 2006 from the donated gowns. Marisa told a reporter for the *Washington Post,* "The drive has really given the girls hope. They'll be able to look back on prom as a point where they were just able to be 17- and 18-year-old girls and be able, in that moment, to forget about what's going wrong."

"You have single-handedly saved prom for countless girls."

—Christina Luwisch, senior class president, Cabrini High School in New Orleans, to Marisa West, coordinator of a prom dress drive after Hurricane Katrina, 2006

"MAGIC IN THE ROOM"

In 2015 several high school juniors and seniors reached out to fellow students who might not have been able to go to prom. For example, one girl, Kaitlin McCarthy, a high school junior in Canton, Massachusetts, invited her friend Matty Marcone to prom. Matty has special needs and many medical problems. Kaitlin didn't do it because she felt sorry for Matty. She did it because Matty is her friend and she wanted to include him at the dance. And the whole school helped her out, including her boyfriend. Teachers were there to help Matty with his diabetes medication, and the hockey team made sure he had many people to talk to. Matty and Kaitlin were even crowned prom king and queen. "There was magic in the room that night" said Matty's mom, who attended as a chaperone.

Another example of goodwill and inclusiveness happened at Division Avenue High School in Levittown, New York. Sarah Kardonsky, a senior, invited Michael Pagano to prom. Michael has autism and wanted to go to prom but was turned down by several girls. Sarah arranged a promposal that involved reaching out to Michael's favorite professional football team, the New York Jets. Members of the team sent videos of themselves saying that Sarah wanted to go to prom with Michael. Sarah arranged for the videos to be shown in school during the daily announcements. Michael was thrilled—and accepted Sarah's invitation.

Sarah's promposal garnered so much publicity that it led to a guest appearance on the *Ellen DeGeneres Show* daytime talk show. But Sarah did not get caught up in the media hype. She kept a healthy perspective, commenting that "people who worry so much about what dress to wear or who to go with, that's not what prom is about. Prom is about having a good time. You should just be surrounded by people who make you happy."

CHAPTER FIVE

TWENTY-SOMETHINGS:
TIPS FOR A FUN, SAFE PROM

Prom can be an exciting, positive experience where teens see one another at their best—dressed up, happy, and having fun. Prom often gives a heady sense of nostalgia and independence—staying out all night; knowing that high school is ending; knowing that the new chapter of young adulthood is just around the corner; and

> "The mother of excess is not joy but joylessness."
>
> —*Friedrich Nietzsche,* Human, All Too Human, *Aphorism 77, 1878*

knowing that some high school friendships will endure, while some will fade. Prom can be a time to seize the moment, to make an indelible, fun, beautiful memory of high school.

But prom can have a dark side. Prom can be filled with pressure and expectations that create anxiety, dread, and confusion—for both girls and boys. Prom can be an event where teens become dangerously inebriated at unsupervised pre-parties and after-parties. Prom can be a time when a girl is expected to have sex with her date, even if this is against her will. Being reckless is often born of insecurity and pain. Teens who genuinely feel good about themselves and their friendships don't have to get wasted to have a great time at prom.

If you are feeling insecure at prom, losing control of good judgment won't help you feel more confident in the long run. It's better to stay grounded and safe. If you think you might need help with fear, anxiety, or depression, reach out to someone— your parents, a therapist, a teacher, a doctor, or another trusted adult—for help and support. You can also check out the resources at the back of this book.

REFLECTIONS ON PROM

Here are some reflections from twenty-somethings who attended their proms. Some of them had good times at prom. Some of them had challenging experiences and hard choices to make at their proms and after-parties. Some have opinions about what prom means in the big picture of life. All of them share intelligent, inspiring insights and tips. (All names and other identifying information have been changed to protect identity, unless otherwise specified.)

MARY

I went to prom for my sophomore, junior, and senior years. Each time it was with a guy that I was either interested in or dating. I think historically there has been such an emphasis put on senior prom and a pressure to make it the best night of high school, but for me personally it was very underwhelming.

Though I don't personally have any horror stories to share, as my experiences were PG, one of my good friends was put in a very compromising situation. Prom at my school is only for juniors and seniors, but upperclassmen can ask down. Sophomore year, my friend was asked by an older boy who had a reputation as being very pushy and forceful. She was very nervous and frightened about what he was going to do on the day of the dance. Though many people warned her that maybe sitting this dance out might be the safest option, she decided to go anyway.

At her prom after party, the boy became very intoxicated and began to follow her around the party. He continued to try to get her to come into a room with him and was frighteningly persistent. After my friend put off his advances, the boy went around the party loudly exclaiming that "she's a younger girl, she's obligated to hook up with me." The older girls at the party took my friend under their wing to help her fend him off. They were so kind and incredibly understanding of her situation. I respect my friend for holding her ground and not giving into the pressure of the moment. The lessons I took away from her experiences were to either opt out of attending if the boy who asks you to prom makes you uncomfortable, and also to tell your peers if you feel unsafe or that you need help avoiding a compromising situation.

> "I respect my friend for holding her ground and not giving into the pressure of the moment."
>
> —Mary

ALEXA

The problem with prom is the huge buildup about it. It's supposed to be the celebration for four years of hard work. There's an expectation to feel a sense of camaraderie with your graduating classmates, that it's supposed to be the best night of high school. Anything with that much expectation is sure to be problematic. There is also such an emphasis on the way you look. People spend weeks beforehand finding the right dress, the right shoes, the right date. I remember feeling, *This is as young as I am ever going to be. These are the pictures I'll show my grandkids.* That's kind of the feeling you get from the hours of photos and preparations. I really dreaded the whole event, because I knew even before it began that it wouldn't be what we were told it was going to be—some kind of perfect night. I didn't predict it was going to go as badly as it did, though.

" One of my favorite parts, speeding through the beautiful city, not yet having arrived, just the anticipation. Like holding a wrapped present before you open it."

—Alexa

My experience of prom: spending hours in high heels posing uncomfortably in someone's multi-million dollar house by the beach. I didn't really feel close to the people in my prom group, which was also a huge stressor. If you're not naturally a person who has a group, you suddenly feel pressure to choose one to take photos with. My best friends were spread out, and so many of the people in the photos (when I look back on them) I didn't know well at all. I wore this dark blue dress, and I remember everyone also coincidentally wearing blue dresses. We took a limo to Navy Pier [an entertainment venue on Lake Michigan in Chicago, Illinois], which was where our prom was located, blasting music the whole time. That was probably one of my favorite parts, speeding through the beautiful city, not yet having arrived, just the anticipation. Like holding a wrapped present before you open it.

When we got to prom, most of the time was spent commenting on the way people look. I remember comparing myself to everyone, which I don't think I would necessarily do now. People did look stunningly beautiful, but it became exhausting to say to every girl you saw, "Oh my god, you're so beautiful, look at you! I love your dress!" I don't think guys had the same experience whatsoever. They all wore variations of the same outfit.

Prom itself was a lot of dancing. There were fireworks that went off at one point, and I remember looking around and seeing our entire grade looking up at the sky. Some people were holding hands. That moment, that's when I felt a sense of camaraderie.

After prom, my boyfriend and I went to get our bags (we were planning to sleep over at a friends' house who was hosting an after-party), and they were sitting in a corner. The dean [of the high school] was standing there, asking us if these were our bags. I said yes, and she pulled out an empty plastic bag that smelled like weed from my boyfriend's backpack, and an empty one hitter [for smoking marijuana]. She basically was like, you have to call your parents to come get you, and you can't go on the prom boat (our class after-party). I just broke down crying, I was so mad and humiliated, especially because I wasn't even the one who brought those things. Meanwhile, my boyfriend was pleading with the dean, who was threatening that I couldn't walk at graduation. I had never gotten in trouble before, and I cried the whole ride home. Prom was this huge buildup for maybe one of the worst nights of all time.

I think my best advice about prom would be: stay in the moment. Don't assign it any more weight than just a fun party with friends. It holds this immense amount of gravity in our culture, and it's really hard to have fun if all you can think about is how much fun it's supposed to be. Also, I would say that the best moments of high school were not the ones in which posed photos were taken, where hundreds of dollars were spent, where you were expected to stay up all night binge drinking [or] losing your virginity.

The best moments of high school were spontaneous and

casual. Running through a rainstorm with my best friend. Watching the sunrise with my boyfriend. Hours spent at a local cafe slaving over a [math] problem set. Those moments were so much better and more meaningful. My high school experience wasn't summarized or determined by prom, even though that's how I felt that night.

LARA

Lara offers an informative list of her observations about prom. They include these points:

POSITIVES

- [Prom is] a night to remember as a part of my high school years where the school can come together for a good time.
- An opportunity to be fancy and dress up and not wear the uniform that was mandatory at my private school.
- A day in which I was able to treat myself to beauty-related activities such as mani-pedi and getting my hair done.
- Taking pictures with my best friends all looking our best.
- Picking out a dress that I felt like a princess in and felt confident.
- Enjoying time with friends or a significant other in a setting that was atypical.
- Taking a party bus, going to a fancy hotel, feeling very special.

NEGATIVES

- Stress due to planning the venues for pictures and after-party, sorting out transportation.
- Stress and drama regarding picking the people to be in the group, as not everyone can always fit in the same group and some people felt left out.

- Hostility and fights with friends over prom dates, groups, and plans that cause hurt.
- Dealing with plans falling through.
- Financial aspects that come with prom, as it is an expensive event.
- Trying to be understanding and accommodating to the needs and limits of the whole group.

TIPS

- Make sure the work of planning is not all on one person. Divide responsibilities among a few friends to make it more enjoyable and less overwhelming.
- Make sure everyone in the group is on the same page.
- Keep parents in the loop about all plans so there are no surprises.
- If someone in the group is not comfortable with part of the plan, it is fine if they make other arrangements for afterwards. Not everyone has to do the same thing for the whole night.
- The idea that a lake house or vacation house is necessary for the prom after party is not true. This is not needed for a good time and often leads to more complications than necessary. Going to someone's house for a small party can still be a great time. I did this for all three proms that I went to.
- Just because someone asked you to prom does not mean you are obligated to do anything that you feel uncomfortable doing. A good date will be respectful. If your or a friend's date is being inappropriate, you do not have to stay with them and hang out with them during the night.
- It is not necessary to go to prom with someone you are involved with or have a romantic interest in. From personal

experience, it is often more fun to go with a friend.

- Remember at the end of the day that this isn't the biggest, most important event of your life. If everything isn't perfect, as long as you're in good company, it will be a good time.
- Like always, keep an eye on friends to make sure that they are OK and comfortable and having a good time.
- Renttherunway.com is a great option if you want to rent a great dress on a budget. Highly recommended.

"The Eternal Scheme of Things"

Jordan Spencer Cunningham says this of prom, on his website Nerdology.org:

If you're a girl who didn't get asked, you are beautiful and worth it just the way you are—you're probably more beautiful than most girls who did get asked, quite honestly; the "world," as we call it, doesn't look at the true beauty each girl has but only outward beauty . . . in spite of what you may think and what society is subtly trying to make you think, not going to prom has approximately a zero percent chance of affecting the rest of your life for good or bad. You still have great value. You are not worthless. You are not sub-standard. You are not broken. Whatever your social status is, please ignore it. However many friends you have right now, it doesn't matter. Whether you've gone to no high school dances or a thousand of them, your worth is not affected either way.

> "Whether you've gone to no high school dances or a thousand of them, your worth is not affected either way."

The same goes for . . . boys. You have no obligation to ask anyone out to any dance . . . a . . . high school dance is nothing in the eternal scheme of things. Maybe you want to ask a girl but you're afraid. Maybe you're just too nervous. Maybe you're not ready. Maybe you have absolutely no interest but feel pressure from society and culture. [Remember] . . . you'll be just fine . . . even if you never, ever ask anyone to a dance.

CARRIE

I went to two proms, my junior year and senior year of high school. For junior year, I went with my boyfriend at the time. He was two years older than I was and was in his first year of college. I went with a small group of friends. I enjoyed getting all dressed up and going to the dance. I had bought a dress while on college visits, so I knew it was unique and something special.

I remember being disappointed because my boyfriend wasn't very interested in dancing and was pretty negative and stand-offish most of the time. (He did break up with me shortly after prom. I think he wasn't really into me at prom either but didn't want to leave me stranded.) I made the best of the dance, but I do remember feeling let down that it wasn't everything I had hoped it would be. I did not go to any after-prom activities, as I was performing in a big choir event the next morning. I went home following the dance to get sleep.

" Be true to yourself and do what you enjoy doing. Try not to give in to the social pressures (including taking a date or even dancing with your date!)."

—Carrie

For my senior year, I wasn't planning on attending prom at all. However, a few weeks prior to the dance, a good friend asked me to go as friends. I went and had a nice time. I took this one much less formally and wore an old dress and did my hair myself. I had a nice time with my friends.

I was a pretty straight-laced kid and tended to avoid any of the problems associated with prom. I remember some people had limos and were drinking and partying, but it wasn't my crowd. I avoided that kind of thing. I loved to dance and that was the main draw for me.

Going with the Flow

Rob says that his tip about prom is to go with a group. High school should be about making connections with your friends. Don't worry about impressing just one person. He also encourages teens not to care so much about things being perfect. Be OK with plans changing and go with the flow. Have fun with your good friends.

The biggest tip I have is to be true to yourself and do what you enjoy doing. Try not to give in to the social pressures (including taking a date or even dancing with your date!). If the people you are with have a negative attitude, that is contagious. Find the people that are enjoying themselves and have fun with them.

STACY

At my high school, we had a junior prom. The juniors planned it and hosted it, and the seniors were also allowed to attend. My junior prom was way more fun than my senior prom, and it all had to do with the people that I went with. Junior year I went with my boyfriend. We had been dating since eighth grade, so it was expected that we went together. We went to the prom with three other couples. It was a really fun group of people! We rented a limo that took us to the prom location, which was about an hour away. Our parents all chipped in for the limo.

I don't remember too much about the actual dance itself. The fun part for me was after the dance. Our school had a post-prom party in the school field house that started right after the dance ended and lasted until about 3 am. They had fun games, food, and a hypnotist, which was really fun to watch. After the post-prom party, my whole prom group went to my friend's house and spent the rest of the night in her hot tub. It was really fun getting back to her house and changing into our swimsuits, prom hair and makeup still intact. We probably only got about two hours of sleep before we woke up and had a big pancake brunch.

One of the best parts of my junior prom was that it initiated some really great friendships. When we were organizing prom groups a few weeks before prom, our group kind of randomly came together. The guys were all good friends, but the girls weren't very close with each other or with the guys. After prom night, we became such a close group of friends all through the rest of high school. One of the guys that was in our group and I became so close that he stood up in my wedding. It was a fun night where we were able to just talk, hang out, and really get to know each other. It was a small little party that just strengthened our friendships.

"After prom night, we became such a close group of friends all through the rest of high school."

—Stacy

My advice would be to make sure you end up somewhere that you know and have been to before so you feel comfortable. Also, I would make sure to be with a group of people that you know are going to make good decisions. Going out with the party crowd will most likely get you in trouble.

JONATHAN

Like Lara, Jonathan has a helpful list of positives and negatives to consider. He says this about prom:

POSITIVES

- I went to a very large and diverse public school (more than nine hundred kids in my graduating class), so seeing everyone together in one room and dressed to the nines was both impressive and really wonderful to see. Egos were, for the most part, dropped, and everyone just wanted to have a good time.

- Despite not getting to go with my friends, I actually ended up meeting a lot of new people and making new friends. Socializing in high school can be so hard because of the phony-hierarchy of cliques. Surprisingly this all went away at prom and people put down whatever walls they had up.
- Silly as it sounds, I'm proud to have my awkward prom photos. Everyone gets them and they all become dated and incredibly awkward no matter what your age. I suppose this is a hindsight "positive" but I love having these photos to look back.
- Another hindsight "positive": After living overseas for a couple of years [I quickly learned] how American a tradition prom is. People from other countries ask a lot of questions and are envious of prom. At the time of my prom, I wasn't completely enthusiastic about dressing up, paying a lot of money, and dancing in front of my class, but now I'm strangely proud of this cultural tradition we have and am really glad I went.
- It's a party. Sounds obvious, but there's so much hype and pressure that people forget it's a party. Beyond whatever weight the word *prom* has, at the end of the day, it's a gigantic party that all my friends were going to. That doesn't happen very often in life and even if the party were a disaster, it's always fun to hang out with your friends, all dressed up.

NEGATIVES

- Shortly before prom, I started dating a girl from a different social circle, so I ended up going and sitting with her friends and knew no one in my party. It wasn't terrible, they were nice, but I had to watch all my best friends sitting together across the room for the first few hours. Once dancing started, we all got to hang out.

- The food and some dancing were in a ballroom, but then everyone was led to one of two mid-sized cruises that went out onto Lake Michigan. These boats were uncomfortable, and the bathroom could only service two people at a time. (There were a few hundred people on each boat.)
- The food was terrible. Some proms don't offer food and students go to dinner beforehand and have fun.
- The drunk people, oh the drunk people. Not surprisingly students used this opportunity to get drunk, and a good amount of people were caught and taken out of prom. It hurt them a lot more than it helped them. They embarrassed themselves and instead of looking cool, most of them cried and had to tell their parents and weren't allowed to walk at their graduation.
- No one really looks good in a tuxedo. Maybe James Bond, but I think that's still a pretty big maybe.[59]

"No one really looks good in a tuxedo. Maybe James Bond, but I think that's still a pretty big maybe."

— Jonathan

BEN

I ended up going to prom with my ex-girlfriend. I dated her all senior year and then she dumped me. I was devastated at the time. I was worried about the plans and about how it would be to go with her since we had broken up. It ended up just working out. We had a talk and agreed that we should just have a fun evening. This put me at ease and set up the whole night to be a really fun celebration. Now when I look back on it, prom was a culmination of spending four years with really great people and was a way to celebrate that in a festive way. Prom is a high school rite of passage that we all went through together and it was really fun.

I was prom king. It was really interesting because in pop culture you have the idea that the prom king should be the top athlete, football captain, tall, and handsome. I'm not an athlete, I'm short, and in terms of looks, I'm a pretty regular guy. When they announced me as prom king, I saw my twin brother emerge [from among] the tables. He was there cheering for me and took a picture. We still have that picture. I got a crown and I had to wear it the entire evening. It was heavy. People I didn't even know were congratulating me. It was a cool moment in my life.

I was not a drinker in high school. I never had a sip of alcohol, weed, or cigarettes and that didn't change at prom. There is this idea that everyone gets wasted on prom night. That wasn't true for me at all, and I think that wasn't true for a lot of other kids that night.

My general message is that I feel like people get caught up in what is expected, like this is what I'm supposed to do. But in reality, more often than not, no one cares about what anyone else is doing. People just want to go and have a good time.

My advice is to just be you. Don't feel pressured by anyone else to drink or do drugs. Don't do anything you're not comfortable doing just because you think someone wants you to. Just be yourself.

EMMY

I went to my senior prom. I transferred high schools going into my junior year so I decided not to go to prom with the high school I was attending. Instead, I went to my first high school's prom. I didn't go with a boyfriend or significant other but rather with one of my best friends at the time. It was a surprise to my other friends in our friend group who had no idea I was coming.

I didn't mind not going with a significant other, but I do know that it can be pretty nerve racking if one DOES, and that it's even more nerve racking WAITING and WONDERING if you'll be asked. At the prom I went to, some girls were there with guys, others just went with friends. But it's important for girls to know that they can have a great time even if they don't go with a guy. I personally enjoyed not going with a guy because then I didn't have to impress anyone or spend too much time worrying about the dress, hair, and makeup. And I got to spend all my time with my friends and didn't have to worry about entertaining a date.

The dress part is difficult because there are rules for what style is in, and girls get very possessive over their dresses. Sometimes girls start Facebook groups to post pictures of their dress to make sure no one else has the same one. The best thing I did was wear a dress I already had. That way I didn't have to go out and spend money on a dress I likely wouldn't wear again. But I also recommend buying a dress you could potentially see yourself wearing again.

There are MANY preconceived notions about prom night involving sex, drugs, and alcohol. It can seem like everyone is having sex, drinking, or doing drugs. Don't get involved because it seems like everyone else is. In reality, it's a much smaller group (that drinks, etc.) than everyone thinks. Be smart about what you do, where you go, and with whom you go pre- and post-prom. Have all plans and details worked out with your prom partner/ group you're going with. Take advantage of your high school's post-prom offerings.

You want to have a memorable prom, everyone does. The best way to ensure an evening of memories is by staying safe.

CREATING YOUR OWN PROM

As I put the finishing touches on this book, I thought of all the people I talked to, young and old, about their prom experiences. Most of these people had fun experiences at prom, which I hope is true for you as well.

However, one woman raised some thoughtful questions: What if you, like many teens, are not asked to prom? What if a person you like asks someone else? What if you don't have a group of friends to go with? What if you aren't interested in going to prom in the first place? How do you deal with these experiences—are they a disappointment or a relief or a combination of many different feelings? This book includes great insights from teens and young adults on these issues and about how to create proms that are inclusive. And yet the woman, almost a century wise, who shared her memories of proms in the 1930s gave me the most illuminating perspective. She informed me that many happy, successful people never went to their prom.

With this in mind, I hope that if you choose to go to prom, it is a safe, festive celebration that joyfully culminates your high school experience. And if you don't attend your prom, by choice or by chance, remember that a high school prom experience is not required for a bright, even glowing, future.

SOURCE NOTES

6   Jacob Goldstein and Dan Kedme, "Great Moments in 1% History," *New York Times*, May 6, 2012, http://query.nytimes.com/gst/fullpage.html?res=9A0DE2DE113BF935A35756C0A9 649D8B63.

8   Ann Anderson, *High School Prom: Marketing, Morals, and the American Teen* (Jefferson, NC: McFarland, 2012), n.p.

8   Ibid., 8.

9   Ibid., 7–8.

9   Anonymous ninety-nine-year-old woman, e-mail to author, June 9, 2015.

11   Anderson, *High School Prom*, 19.

12–13   Deana Case, "1950's Prom Dresses," *LoveToKnow*, accessed May 12, 2015, http://teens .lovetoknow.com/1950%27s_Prom_Dresses.

14   Anderson, *High School Prom*, 23.

19   Ibid., 64.

22   Beth J. Harpaz, "Proms Evolve from Night of Dressed-Up Romance to Platform for Good Deeds, Social Change," *Huffington Post*, last modified July 10, 2015, http://www .huffingtonpost.ca/2015/04/20/proms-evolve-from-night-o_n_7101102.html.

22   Ibid.

23   "Ask Early!," PromsPlus!, last modified November 1, 2007, http://www.promsplus.com /promadvisor.php.

23   Clemence Michallon, "Pennsylvania Catholic High School Student Who Got Thrown Out of Her Own Prom Because She Wore a Suit Instead of a Dress Attends a Dance at a Different High School," *DailyMail.com*, May 22, 2016, http://www.dailymail.co.uk/news /article-3603014/Aniya-Wolf-got-thrown-prom-Bishop-McDevitt-High-School-Harrisburg -wore-suit-attends-dance-William-Penn-Senior-High-School.html.

26   Miriam Jordan, "What's a Bigger Deal Than Prom These Days? The 'Promposal,'" *Wall Street Journal*, April 4, 2014, http://www.wsj.com/articles/SB1000142405270230384780457947 7512545113716.

27   Emanuella Grinberg, "'Promposal' Pressure Is Intense for Teens," *CNN.com*, May 1, 2014, http://www.cnn.com/2014/05/01/living/promposal-pressure-proms/.

27   Maya Kaufman, "15 Teens Discuss Modern Proms and Promposals," *The Cut*, May 15, 2013, http://nymag.com/thecut/2013/05/15-teens-discuss-modern-prom-and-promposals.html.

28   Stacy Teicher, Khadaroo, "Prom Draft Girls Should Stand Up to Boys Ranking Them, Experts Say," *Christian Science Monitor*, May 7, 2014, http://www.csmonitor.com/USA /Society/2014/0507/Prom-draft-girls-should-stand-up-to-boys-ranking-them-experts-say -video.

29 Jessica Press, "Black + White," *Seventeen*, May 2009, 136–39.

30 Brooke A. Masters, "Heidi and Missy, College Sweethearts," *Washington Post*, March 7, 1994, http://www.washingtonpost.com/archive/lifestyle/1994/03/07/heidi-and-missy-college-sweethearts/9aa0ab12-bde6-42ef-9dc7-3bb5e7139d87/.

31 Jeff Truesdell, "All Girls Dream about Prom," *People.com*, March 29, 2010, http://www.people.com/people/archive/article/0,,20353660,00.html.

32 Tony Merevick, "Couple Plans Own Prom after Student Says School Barred Her from Bringing Her Transgender Boyfriend," *BuzzFeed*, April 15, 2014, http://www.buzzfeed.com/tonymerevick/couple-plans-own-prom-after-student-says-school-barred-her-f#.tuQ1gK1r1.

33 Ibid.

33 Curtis M. Wong, "This Gay Teen Couple from West Virginia Couldn't Have Asked for a More Perfect Prom Night," *HuffingtonPost*, April 29, 2015, http://www.huffingtonpost.com/2015/04/29/west-virginia-gay-prom-couple_n_7171984.html.

34 Ibid.

34 Anna Morena, "Transgender Teen Voted Prom Queen at Renton HS," *king5.com*, accessed April 6, 2016, http://www.king5.com/story/news/local/2015/06/07/local-transgende-teen-is-prom-queen-hopeful/28654611/.

34 Ibid.

36 Elizabeth Holmes, "Promoting One-of-a-Kind Looks, Shops Keep Prom Dress Registries," *Wall Street Journal*, April, 1, 2015, http://www.wsj.com/articles/promoting-one-of-a-kind-looks-shops-keep-prom-dress-registries-1427937210.

36 Ibid.

37 Bradley Ryder, "Kyemah McEntyre Revenge," *Inquisitr*, June 10, 2015, http://www.inquisitr.com/2159837/kyemah-mcentyre-prom-dress-from-bullied-teen-an-epic-payback-to-haters/.

37 Helin Jung, "18-Year-Old Who Designed Her Own Prom Dress Is Now Creating Red Carpet Gowns for Celebs," *Cosmopolitan,* June 29, 2015, http://www.cosmopolitan.com/style-beauty/fashion/news/a42678/kyemah-mcentyre-designs-naturi-naughton-bet-awards-dress/.

39 Annabel Fenwick Elliott, "From Trash to Treasure," *DailyMail.com*, June 9, 2014, 2015, http://www.dailymail.co.uk/femail/article-2653204/From-trash-treasure-High-school-student-paints-Van-Goghs-Starry-Night-40-thrift-store-gown-create-dream-prom-dress.html.

39 Rebecca Irvine, "High School Senior Hand Paints Prom Dress," *KSL.com*, May 23, 2014, http://www.ksl.com/?nid=1010&sid=30001797.

39 Sadie Whitelocks, "Dad to the Rescue! Military Man Hones Sewing Skills So Daughter Can Go to Prom Wearing 'Dream' Camouflage-Inspired Dress," *DailyMail.com*, May 2, 2013, http://www.dailymail.co.uk/femail/article-2318405/Dad-rescue-Military-man-hones-sewing-skills-daughter-prom-wearing-dream-camouflage-inspired-dress.html.

39 "Military Dad Makes Daughter a Camouflage Prom Dress," *FoxNews.com*, May 2, 2013, http://www.foxnews.com/us/2013/05/02/military-dad-makes-daughter-camouflage-prom-dress.html.

42 Nell Scovell, "Girl, It Was Scandalous!," *New York Times Magazine*, June 24, 2001, 2016, http://www.nytimes.com/2001/06/24/magazine/24STYLE.html.

42 Ibid.

44 "Free Formal Wear Offered to More Than 1,000 Underprivileged Teens in South LA for Prom, Graduation," *CBSLA.com*, April 10, 2015, http://losangeles.cbslocal.com/2015/04/10/free-formal-wear-offered-to-more-than-1000-underprivileged-teens-in-south-la/.

47 Muriel Clark, "Hay Springs . . . Donating Prom Savings to Haiti," *Nebraska Outback*, February 2, 2010, http://www.outbacknebraska.com/2010/02/hay-springs-nebraska-high-school.html.

47 Melanie Wieseler, "Prom with a Purpose," *Guideposts* 65, no.4 (June 2010): 20.

47 Clark, "Hay Springs."

47–48 Taylor Pittman, "Texas Prom-Goers Wouldn't Let a Car Accident or a Wheelchair Ruin Their Plans," *HuffPost Teen*, March 27, 2015, http://www.huffingtonpost.com/2015/03/27/alyah-mitchell-brings-prom-to-hospital_n_6955760.html.

48 Matt Murray, "Teen Brings Prom to the Hospital after Her Date Was Injured in Car Crash," *NBC Today*, March 29, 2015, http://legacy.11alive.com/story/news/2015/03/29/teen-brings-prom-texas-hospital-after-her-date-was-injured/70644342.

49 Alicia Dennis, "Two Friends Save Prom," *People.com*, May 31, 2010, http://www.people.com/people/archive/article/0,,20387212,00.html.

49 Joe Clark, "That Cinderella Thing Teachers' Aid Makes Prom Night Memorable," *Philly.com*, May, 10, 1999, http://articles.philly.com/1999-05-10/news/25514746_1_prom-night-senior-prom-first-prom.

49 Ibid.

50 Ibid.

50 Ann Brenoff, "Senior Citizens Show They Can Still Cut a Rug at College Prom," *HuffPost 50*, April 9, 2015, http://www.huffingtonpost.com/2015/04/09/senior-citizens-college-prom_n_7033572.html.

50 Ibid.

51 Bill Hewitt and Kate Kliss, "A Time to Dance," *People.com*, May 24, 1999, http://www.people.com/people/archive/article/0,,20128319,00.html.

52 Annie Gowan, "2,800 Prom Gowns from a Single Thread," *Washington Post*, May 12, 2006, http://www.washingtonpost.com/wp-dyn/content/article/2006/05/11/AR2006051102258.html.

52 Ibid.

53 Beth J. Harpaz, "Some Teens Using Proms as Platforms for Good Deeds, Social Change," *New Haven Register*, April 20, 2015, http://www.nhregister.com/article/NH/20150420 /NEWS/150429972

53 Beth J. Harpaz, "For Some, Prom Is a Platform for Good Deeds, Social Change," *Online Athens*, April 26, 2015, http://onlineathens.com/local-news/2015-04-26/some-prom-platform-good -deeds-social-change.

53 Ibid.

54 Friedrich Nietzsche, "Human, All Too Human," trans. by R. J.Hollingdale (Cambridge: Cambridge University Press, 1996), 230.

55–56 High school graduate #1, e-mail to author, July 6, 2015.

56–59 High school graduate #2, e-mail to author, August 2, 2015.

59–61 High school graduate #3, e-mail to author, November 2, 2015.

61 Jordan Spencer Cunningham, "I'm Not Going to Prom–Am I a Loser? Answers to the Lifelong Question," *Nerdology.org* (blog), February 23, 2013, 2-23-13, http://nerdology.org/2013/02 /im-not-going-to-prom-am-i-a-loser-answers-to-the-lifelong-question/.

62–63 High school graduate #4, e-mail to author, August 16, 2015.

63 High school graduate #5, personal conversation with author, November 22, 2015.

63–64 High school graduate #6, e-mail to author, August 17, 2015.

64–66 High school graduate #7, e-mail to author, January 3, 2016.

66–67 High school graduate #8, e-mail to author, November 8, 2015.

67–68 High school graduate #9, e-mail to author, November 11, 2015.

SELECTED BIBLIOGRAPHY

Anderson, Ann. *High School Prom: Marketing, Morals, and the American Teen.* Jefferson, NC: McFarland, 2012.

Best, Amy. *Prom Night: Youth, Schools, and Popular Culture.* New York: Routledge, 2000.

Marling, Karal Ann. *Debutante: Rites and Regalia of American Debdom.* Lawrence: University Press of Kansas, 2004.

Post, Emily. *Etiquette in Society, in Business, in Politics and at Home.* New York: Funk & Wagnalls, 1922. http://www.gutenberg.org/files/14314/14314-h/14314-h.htm#CHAPTER_XVIII.

Rollin, Lucy. *Twentieth-Century Teen Culture by the Decades.* Westport, CT: Greenwood, 1999.

FURTHER INFORMATION

Books

Fithen, Hunter. *102 Memorable and Manly Ways to Ask a Lady to Prom.* North Charleston, SC: CreateSpace Independent Publishing, 2013.

Metz, Lauren. *The Prom Book: The Only Guide You'll Ever Need.* San Francisco: Zest Books, 2013.

Spillman, Rob. *The Time of My Life: Writers on the Heartbreak, Hormones, and Debauchery of the Prom.* New York: Broadway Books, 2008.

Websites and Videos

"Full Face Prom Makeup Tutorial: Manny Mua"—YouTube
https://www.youtube.com/watch?v=-PpQ9E_dJLA
Makeup can be for everyone! Self-described "boy beauty vlogger" Manna Mua walks you through a chic prom makeup look.

"Glamorous & Simple Prom 2016 Makeup Tutorial!"—YouTube
https://www.youtube.com/watch?v=7fGWB1_j3Zg
This video is a prom makeup tutorial made in Spring 2016.

"The Guys' Guide to Prom: Tips on Style, Social Graces"—*Pittsburgh Post-Gazette*
http://www.post-gazette.com/life/fashion/2014/04/07/The-guys-guide-to-prom
/stories/201404070011
This is a good walk-through to read before prom. This article discusses cell phone etiquette while at prom and points out that your date may or may not welcome chivalry. The site also includes potential websites and sources for men's prom wear.

"Here Is 1 Simple Trick to Help You Choose the Perfect Prom Dress for Your Body Type!"—*PromStyling.com*
http://www.promstyling.com/perfect-prom-dress-for-my-body-type/
Identify your body type and learn about which prom dress styles will be particularly flattering on you and what you might want to avoid.

"How to Dress for Prom: A Young Man's Guide to Formal Menswear"—Real Men Real Style
   http://www.realmenrealstyle.com/how-to-dress-for-prom/
   This page walks you through several options for guys at prom. It includes a video by someone from
   Real Men Real Style, further explaining how to look your best on prom night.

"How to Have an Epic Prom—without Being Asked"—*TigerBeat*
   http://tigerbeat.com/video/how-to-have-an-epic-prom-without-being-asked/
   In a video, Laura Marano walks you through how to have a fun time at prom, date or no date.

"It's Our Prom: A Night to De-Gender, Celebrating Gay and Transgendered Teens at Prom"—*MTV*
   http://www.mtv.com/news/interactive/breaking-prom-gender-rules/
   Check out this cool MTV link for photos and stories from teens who defy gender norms and who
   have participated in their proms as their true selves.

"Mareshia Rucker on Being Featured at Human Rights Museum"—*CBS News*
   http://www.cbc.ca/player/play/2522883120
   This short news video features Mareshia Rucker, an organizer of the first racially integrated prom
   at Wilcox County High School in Georgia and the girl who donated her prom dress to the Canadian
   Human Rights Museum.

"Prom Dresses through the Years: An Evolution"—*Elle*
   http://www.elle.com/fashion/g26089/evolution-of-prom-dresses/
   Feeling retro? Peruse the classy and cringeworthy prom fashions of yesteryears in this slide show.
   The site is potentially a great tool for finding dress inspiration!

"Prom Makeup Tutorial (Mainly Drugstore)"—YouTube
   https://www.youtube.com/watch?v=R8SWTQjVHdc
   This is a fun and pretty makeup tutorial, from Lauren Curtis, using mostly drugstore brands. Don't
   break the bank!

Prom Section—*Seventeen*
   http://www.seventeen.com/prom-dresses/
   A staple of every year's prom season, *Seventeen*'s prom section online shares the newest trends,
   steals and deals, and includes quizzes to help you figure out what you really want at prom.

Prom Section—*Teen Vogue*
   http://www.teenvogue.com/prom
   Another prom season essential, *Teen Vogue*'s prom section has inspiring fashion photographs,
   quizzes, and more.

"Prom Tips for Guys"—*LoveToKnow*
   http://teens.lovetoknow.com/Prom_Tips_for_Guys
   This is a general guide to prom for guys. This page walks you through the before and after of prom
   and how to make it the best prom it can be.

"6 Natural Hairstyles to Try for Prom"—*Teen Vogue*
   http://www.teenvogue.com/gallery/prom-hairstyles-for-natural-hair
   Rock your natural hair on prom night with these hairdo ideas. Photographs starring celebrities will
   help illustrate the concepts.

"10 Life-Saving Essentials to Pack in Your Prom Clutch"—*Seventeen*
> http://www.seventeen.com/prom/g303/prom-fashion-emergencies/
> Make sure you're prepared for anything at prom! This slide show walks you through the emergency basics you'll want to carry with you on the big day.

"33 Impossibly Gorgeous Prom Hair Ideas"—*BuzzFeed*
> https://www.buzzfeed.com/juliegerstein/impossibly-gorgeous-prom-hair-ideas
> The site shows lovely prom hairstyles for multiple hair types. Diagrams and linked YouTube videos will help you get the picture.

"32 DIY Prom Accessories That Will Make You the Coolest Kid in School"—*BuzzFeed*
> https://www.buzzfeed.com/peggy/cool-and-unexpected-prom-accessories
> These cool and quirky DIY accessories are perfect for those who like to do things a little differently. Learn how to add a cool indie touch to your prom ensemble.

"What Every LGBTQ Teen (and Their School) Needs to Know about Prom"—*Huffington Post*
> http://www.huffingtonpost.com/2014/05/16/lgbt-prom-rights_n_5337169.html
> Use this as a primer on attending prom as a member of the LGBTQ community. Know your rights and view some cute pics of LGBTQ couples on the big night out.

YA Prom Books—*Goodreads*
> http://www.goodreads.com/list/show/2163.YA_Prom_Books
> Check out (and vote on) the best young adult prom books or find one to greet the season.

Resources

All services offered by the organizations on this list are free and support groups are confidential.

Alcohol and Substance Abuse
Alateen (Alcoholics Anonymous for Teens)
http://www.al-anon.alateen.org/for-alateen
888-425-2666, Monday through Friday, 8 a.m. to 6 p.m. (eastern time)
This site is for teens who have or know someone who has a drinking problem.

National Alcohol and Substance Abuse Information Center
http://www.addictioncareoptions.com
800-784-6776, available 24/7
This site can help you find support, resources, and information in your area about substance abuse.

Depression and Suicide Prevention
Depression and Bipolar Support Alliance (DBSA)
http://www.dbsalliance.org
This site offers support, inspiration, and resources to deal with depression and bipolar disorder.

National Suicide Prevention Lifeline
http://www.suicidepreventionlifeline.org
800-273-TALK (8255), available 24/7
This site and the related hotline offer support and information about suicide prevention, education, and other resources in your area. The hotline is staffed 24/7 by trained crisis counselors.

Project Safe Place
http://nationalsafeplace.org/safe-place-teens/
800-RUNAWAY
The website, interactive text option, and national toll-free hotline help teens who are dealing with bullying, sexual identity, eating disorders, crime, drugs and alcohol, and other tough issues. Counselors and volunteers help teens who may be considering running away from home find a safe place to stay.

Eating Disorders
Anorexia Nervosa and Associated Disorders (ANAD) Eating Disorders Helpline
http://www.anad.org
http://anadheop@anad.org
630-577-1330, Monday through Friday, 9 a.m. to 5 p.m. (central standard time)
This site offers compassion and support, plus information about self-help groups and treatment options for people dealing with eating disorders.

National Eating Disorders Association (NEDA) Helpline
http:www.nationaleatingdisorders.org
800-931-2237, Monday through Thursday, 9 a.m. to 9 p.m., Friday, 9 a.m. to 5 p.m. (eastern time)
This site offers compassionate support and information about treatment options for people with eating disorders.

Pregnancy
Planned Parenthood
https://www.plannedparenthood.org/teens
800-230-PLAN or 800-230-7526
This comprehensive site for teens, parents, and educators provides information, counseling, and referrals for individuals who want to better understand human reproduction, dating and sex, sexual and gender identity, sexually transmitted diseases, and birth control.

Rape and Sexual Assault
Rape, Abuse, & Incest National Network (RAINN) Helpline
http://www.rainn.org
800-656-HOPE (4673)
This site offers judgment-free support and guidance, plus information about resources in your area for dealing with the trauma of rape and sexual assault.

Women Organized Against Rape (WOAR) 24-Hour Helpline
http://www.woar.org
215-985-3333, available 24/7
Click on the teen services link at this site to find information about support, education, and other material for survivors of rape and sexual assault.

Sexuality
GLBT National Help Center Youth Talk Line
http://www.glnh.org
800-246-PRIDE (7743)
This site and hotline offer free peer counseling and support for teens dealing with sexuality and gender identity. Information is also available about dealing with bullying, coming out, and practicing safe sex. The

site sponsors a weekly moderated online talk group for transgender teens between the ages of twelve and nineteen.

Sexually Transmitted Diseases (STDs)
Centers for Disease Control and Prevention
http://www.cdc.gov/STD
800-CDC-INFO or 800-232-4636 (English and Spanish)
Specialists provide information at this site for heterosexual and LGBTQ teens and adults about identifying, treating, and preventing a wide range of sexually transmitted diseases.

INDEX

PHOTO ACKNOWLEDGMENTS

ABOUT THE AUTHOR

Jill S. Zimmerman Rutledge, LCSW, is a psychotherapist who has worked with adolescents and adults for more than thirty years. She has lectured nationally on the topics of eating disorders, stress management, and women's body image.

Rutledge has had a long association with Anorexia Nervosa and Associated Disorders (ANAD), an international self-help organization. She is also on the clinical advisory board for HeyUgly, an organization dedicated to improving the self-esteem of youth. She is the advice expert on www.newmoon.com, a website for preadolescent and adolescent girls, and has contributed to Stop-Bullies.com, a website for bullying prevention. She has lectured at the University of Chicago, Loyola University, and Northwestern University and has presented at numerous professional conferences.

Rutledge has been featured in national and international television and radio shows, including ABC News, NPR, MTV-Finland, and the Body Image Revolution Telesummit. She has also been featured in magazines and newspapers, including *YM, Teen People, Fitness, Mothering, Daughters,* the *Chicago Tribune,* the *Arizona Republic,* the *Detroit News,* and numerous parenting website blogs.

She is the author of several articles on women and the media and body image, as well as an article on breast cancer survival. She has published two award-winning self-help books for adolescent girls, *Dealing with the Stuff That Makes Life Tough: The Ten Things That Stress Girls Out and How to Cope with Them* and *Picture Perfect: What You Need to Feel Better about Your Body.* Rutledge maintains a private psychotherapy practice in Avon, Colorado. Check out her website at www.jillzimmermanrutledge.com for more information.